This is a book for active people. I wrote it on the move...

- *on a barge*

- *in numerous airports*

- *throughout the great british transport system*

- *in the car en route to running my first marathon*
  (happily, I put the laptop down for the duration of the 26 miles)

Who? What? Why?

So, you're reading this book to find out how to build and run your own lead generation machine. But, like any other machine, before you build it you'll need a strong foundation (otherwise it's going to plummet through the floor...)

So first we're going to look at:
• The three pillars of marketing.
• How to define your lead generation strategy.
• Understanding the new B2B psychological contract, the new B2B language rules and the new look and feel rules.

Next, it's time to get the lead generation machine set up with some kit to run it on: all the things you should have set up and in place before you build your machine, like a key message guide, a strong clear website, a proposal template and a Customer Relationship Management system.

Then we get to the main event. (Fanfare please...)

I'll describe the four steps of building a lead generation machine:

Step one: Create great content

Step two: Make some buzz

Step three: Generate leads

Step four: Nurture prospects

Increasing your market share starts here.

What is this book and who should read it?

I spend lots of time with growth-focused CEOs (is there any other kind?). Almost every single one has talked about creating a lead generation machine. Almost no one has said "we're alright for leads, thanks". The feeling is that even if there are good leads today, tomorrow's leads are still invisible with no guarantee that they will 'appear'.

In fact, even where leads are plentiful, usually this sets the brain cogs whirring... "if we can turn over X million with this many leads, what could we achieve with a proper lead generation system in place...?"

This is my kind of thinking. The point is not how many leads you have, but how much market potential you are converting.

This book is for:

- businesses who sell things to other businesses (B2Bs)

- complex sales cycles, knowledge based sales – not toner or toilet cleaning services (though both are utterly essential)

- people who mean business – this means people who are prepared to apply effort and creativity to the lead generation challenge and are not looking for the next magic bullet. Be prepared to build something over time.

Who is Onefish Twofish? – and what have we learnt that might help you?

A very short intro to me and my company. I'm Carrie Bedingfield. I set up a business communication and marketing agency when I was 25. I had a big mortgage, no savings and was the main household earner but I managed to turn hard graft and imagination into a serious company in five years. We've never borrowed a penny from the bank. I'm not super-clever and I didn't have a unique idea, but I knew how to create a focused revenue stream by cornering the market and generating and nurturing leads. I had previously worked in a fast-growth and innovative consultancy where I was given lots of responsibility and cut my teeth on real company growth with two very inspirational directors.

My company, Onefish Twofish, helps clients to position and market themselves effectively to other companies. Over the years, we've seen companies succeed and fail at marketing their efforts. The bottom line is the same throughout – only focused, end-to-end, strategically creative marketing gets results. Anything less wastes money and time. You're better off going after great referrals. It's harsh, but it's the truth and I wouldn't want to waste anyone's time by suggesting there is a halfway house. We'll talk more about what this means in practice in just a short while.

Selling to other businesses – why is it so hard?

Most companies find creating a real lead generation machine a huge struggle, unless they sell something truly market leading (and even then it can feel like very hard work).

What's going on? Why does it feel so hard? Are we doing something wrong? Actually, probably not. But the roadmap in this book will help you do things much, much better – and importantly with less pain and stress.

Let's look at what's going on in the industry right now. Health warning: we're getting right to the heart of the matter here and I'm pulling no punches about what we're all up against. But don't flake out on me as these challenges are the same for everyone – and this book is about how to tackle them. The good stuff is coming, so hang in there and get clear about what we need to overcome.

New threats are popping up all over the place... so most markets are getting saturated

Business services is a mature market. The good old players have been inundated by the Corporate Exiters (those leaving big companies through choice or redundancy and setting up their own companies), the New Guns (the natural order where young things take over from the has-beens), the Vertical

Integrators (those trying to eat their clients' or suppliers' lunch by spreading themselves up and down the value chain) and the Web Wonders (those making the most of the possibilities the internet has opened up).

Of the four sets of newcomers, the **Corporate Exiters** can be the least threatening on paper but the most deadly. They own powerful relationships and can be hard to fight off in a competitive pitch. If you've ever gone through an arduous but seemingly transparent bid process only to find that the project is won by a company with a 'pre-existing relationship' with the client, you'll know exactly what I mean.

The **New Guns** have always been around – they are the normal succession order. It's just there are more of them now. We start businesses younger and younger, the power of Generation Y – loosely, those born after 1980 – being that there are few roles they consider themselves too inexperienced for.

Vertical Integrators are nothing new either – though more and more of us are trying to shorten the value chain as much as possible by cutting out the middle man. Ansoff's matrix tells us (as does common sense) that it's much less risky to sell a new product to an existing market than to a new market. If we can grab that market by acquiring a business that already does this, so much the better. The market is now so fluid and our expectations about competition and

co-opetition are so well managed, that it's not difficult for one company to move into our area of the value chain – and we still might have to buy from them to service our own clients! Very frustrating, but it's happening and we have to deal with it.

Web Wonders? They look hard core – all the ability to do what we do, but online (whether this means service delivery, the product itself or the way they source and sell). But we're not fooled. We all need to bring an element of Web Wonder into our own businesses, but there are very, very few companies completely disrupting the market with online technology. When they do, they do it BIG time (think Skype, Google etc). But it's a threat to be considered with care and not tackled with a knee-jerk reaction.

Maybe you've been stung by one or more of these challengers. Perhaps you can see them just a little way off on the horizon? Or better still, perhaps you are one of these challengers! Wherever you sit, knowing the brandscape around you will help you make good decisions about your market.

With more and more suppliers, partners and vendors tackling the same pool of clients (particularly at the pointy end of the pyramid where there is a finite number of large target companies), it's no surprise that the same old positioning and marketing might not yield the growth you're looking for.

And those markets which aren't saturated, are tackling jaded buyers

Even if you're lucky enough to sell something unique or completely new or truly innovative and totally, absolutely needed, it's difficult to pierce through the noise of other less exciting products.

Creating a product or service with actual differentiators does not necessarily correspond to perceived differentiators. In other words, the wonderful points of true differentiation we have spent time and money carefully inserting into our product or service are not always believable to our target market. They've heard the same assertions time and time again. Even more frustratingly, some companies are so skilled at creating perceived differentiators that they win business over those with actual differentiators.

We need to be so focused and so clear about our value proposition (plus prove and substantiate it at every opportunity).

What's more, the range of ways to interact with and win clients is growing exponentially...

Here's the real crunch point. A great piece of direct mail or a telemarketing campaign or an exhibition used to be all it took to generate a pool of leads for sales people or client managers to follow up on. Add to this two crucial factors and suddenly the landscape explodes.

Super-content is now king (delivering value for free via exceptional content) – how and from where is this produced? On a continual basis? Better than the other 101 pieces of content out there? Which is truly relevant and a must-read for your target audience? The mind boggles.

The number of ways to get our message across and engage with potential customers is increasing exponentially – from Twitter, LinkedIn, Facebook, YouTube, forums and other online spaces... to the myriad of publications, events, blogs, awards and webinars/seminars you could target to generate third party endorsement.

The marketing communication landscape is so disaggregated it's untrue. We just cannot do everything (without bringing the business to a grinding halt) and we have to make choices. The Lead Generation Machine is designed to help you create a chain of manageable activities which feed and nourish each other and generate a clear pipeline of new business.

We're more time-poor than ever

If only we had 72 hours in the day, we could make use of all these fantastic, free (kind of) tools which we're told will sky rocket our new business pipeline. The truth is that most of us have less time than we used to. We are making do with fewer marketing resources, tighter budgets and a much higher expectation of 'marketing efficiency' (the return we expect from our time investment). We're less willing to spend money and time building our brand, but expect more from our lead generation than ever before. Administrators are being roped in to tweet and 'link in', MDs are eking blogs out on the train, marketers are stretched thin trying to project manage a raft of integrated online and offline activities.

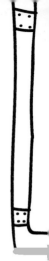

So all-in-all, a bit of a sticky wicket? Actually, no...

Though it's true that we're all struggling to square the circle, there is a huge opportunity. Companies that do this stuff really well, do really well out of it. If it was easy, everyone would be getting it right. The fact that it's challenging means that getting it even half right puts you head and shoulders above your competitors.

It's a huge, huge opportunity to differentiate your organisation and stoke it full of short and long term value while others waste budget and fail to get their collective act together.

The opportunity is yours – take it.

How to use this book

This is a:

- Cook-book
- Idea-book
- Look, make and do book
- Think-aloud-scribble-on-it-then-ask-the-nice-lady-next-to-you-on-the-tube-book

This is not:

- An unbelievable New Technique - YOURS for $99 (special introductory price $95.50), no refunds given.
- A short cut (in fact doing this properly will be hugely challenging, though ultimately and unfailingly rewarding).

With that in mind, I recommend you skim it in one sitting if you can (it's a short-haul flight book, really) and then go back and dig into the sections that are most relevant with a pack of post-it notes and a thick black pen.

Promise me you won't read it, say "Hmm, what a good idea" and then give it back to the colleague who lent it to you. Whatever it sparks for you (and let's face it, the really clever ideas are in your head not mine), *do it, do it, do it.*

My three B2B marketing pillars

If I had to boil down my philosophy on marketing for companies who are not the market leader, it's these three things:

1. Ruthless focus
2. End-to-end approach
3. Strategic creativity

Marketing burns time and money. It's a pure overhead. Yes, a great marketing campaign will make you money, but the cost of making that extra money should be as low as possible. Being the market leader (which most people reading this book won't be) brings with it privileges and responsibilities. If you're not the market leader, you are freed from the responsibility of 'being everywhere' but you must challenge the market leader or your larger competitors by doing things differently and better — not just employing similar tactics on a smaller budget.

Be ruthlessly focused

I have a very small cat. She only weighs around a kilo and a half even though she's nearly seven. If you pick her up, she's light as a feather. But

if she stands on you in the night, it's like someone's dropped a spanner from the ceiling. Why? Because she has tiny, tiny paws. So even her very small weight feels like lead when transferred through her ruthlessly focused paws.

The point is that small comparative weight (turnover, track record, manpower, client list – whatever this might mean for you) can be very powerful indeed if it's sharply focused. Whether you're a start up or a well-established business, we can all learn from this.

Where could a bit of ruthless focus enable you to put real pressure on the marketplace?

Be end to end

Most customers will go on a long journey with you before and after they buy. We know that most businesses need a range of trigger points to start and continue buying from you, from hearing about you in the press to receiving something of value to them, to having a positive conversation (or a positive online experience). And yet we tend to treat lead generation as a one-step process. Get lead, convert it.

Be strategically creative

This is a tough one – but it's absolutely essential. It's the part that connects your brand to your market place with dynamism and impact.

In my experience, there are three types of campaigns.

"Straight down the line" – good solid copy and creative, a clear message, a safe bet.

"Let's do something a bit different" - something creative for the sake of it, grabbing attention purely and simply through being out of the ordinary or going against the grain.

"Strategic creativity" – campaigns which take the essence of the offer and illustrate this vividly through creative content, media or copy.

Put like this, it's easy to see where the first two are going wrong. Perhaps it's harder to visualise what the latter might look like as there are so few good examples of it about. The world of marketing to consumers (business-to-consumer or B2C for short) - is full of good strategic creativity. The B2B world is painfully threadbare.

WHATS THE BIG IDEA?

Here's how we do it at Onefish Twofish.

We pin down:

- What's the problem/solution this campaign solves?
- What's the unequivocal message this campaign is all about?
- What's the big idea?

(My thanks at this stage must go to Steve Harrison who has written an excellent guide to producing truly creative work and articulated this far better than I can here. His book is called How To Do Better Creative Work)

The Big Idea is the essential component that the whole campaign rests on. There can only be one, otherwise the rest of this process will not work (and then you're back to a "straight down the line" campaign which is ok and sometimes necessary, but not nearly as impactful).

We think about how the campaign can embody this Big Idea and bring it to life in every possible way:

- What format would bring it to life?
- What messaging and tone of voice will illustrate the Big Idea?
- What kind of visuals will tell the story?

Very often the simplest executions are the hardest to come up with, but the most powerful and the easiest to translate across all your marketing contact points.

Some examples to mull over...

Strategic creativity at a brand level

The **Xancam** logo is a great example of a big idea brought to life brilliantly in a logo. Xancam is all about strategic, commercial business psychology - specifically, how large organisations can identify and develop people with the potential to be exceptional leaders. The key here is potential. The logo expresses the big idea by transforming the 'X' of Xancam into a window behind which remarkable people images are just visible. The brand concept expresses the idea of something tremendous which is yet to be revealed and the 'X' feels like a star in the night sky - a perfect metaphor for the talent Xancam helps to identify.

4sl Group, a strategic IT services company, has a clean sharp logo - but it's the iconography associated with the brand which tells the story. A brand and positioning workshop revealed a clear point of view for 4sl to take to the market - that successful IT functions have 'TQ", Technical Quotient. Think IQ, but for technology. TQ is a function of cost, performance and risk. 4sl's huge expertise is to help organisations to track and leverage these three items. The creative expresses this expert knowledge by creating an equation in a blackboard chalk style, suggesting intellectual property and deep experience in bringing these three factors together to create a successful IT function.

Strategic creativity at a campaign level

Outsourced recruitment service company, BlueGlue, wanted to tell their market place that its service is the ultra-simple alternative to an expensive recruitment agency. A campaign was designed to empathise with the market's frustration with the cost and hassle of the traditional agency approach and to show that BlueGlue is simple, transparent and a viable alternative route - the new way of doing things. Founder, Bill Ingram, is a big personality.

The big idea was to use the logo marks to represent a) where things go wrong, b) how BlueGlue founder, Bill Ingram, can glue them back together and c) the positive end result. The result was fun, fresh and incredibly clear and the campaign generated incoming phone calls - a big result in a saturated market.

Defining your strategy

I'm big on cornering markets. As marketers and directors, we set ourselves up in too many races we can't possibly win. Coming second (or worse – fifth, tenth or twentieth) is expensive – you're always nibbling away at someone else's lunch. Winning races is very profitable. The more you win, the more you win.

Quick quiz: Try these questions out for size - mark yourself out of 10 and see how well you have cornered a profitable market place.

Do you know exactly how your marketplace breaks down and who you will target?
Have you explicitly staked a claim on that target market and positioned yourself in the most profitable space?
Have you described and substantiated your offering consistently across all media?
Have you clearly and systematically communicated your message to this target market?
Do you have a roadmap for developing and sustaining ownership of this target market?
Does your mark out of ten still stand or do you want to revise it slightly?

If you haven't got a resounding 'yes' to each and every one of these questions, that's good news. There's work to be done and ground to be gained, possibly for free. Excellent.

Cornering the market is all about positioning yourself squarely in the most profitable space and then owning this area of the market, either through:

- What you sell (some of you will be lucky enough to have a unique or innovative product)
- Who you sell it to (some of us can tailor our product for a specific market, making us the owner of that market place, if not the only people selling that product or service)
- Or how you deliver it (this is where it gets really interesting – if you are not one of a kind and don't want to reduce the size of your potential market place, you could find a way to deliver what you do that meets an unmet need for your customers in a way others can't)

Ideas for differentiating 'how' you deliver your product or service:

- Offer some kind of results guarantee or shared risk and reward
- Change the media people can use to buy from you – think about how your customers would ideally like to transact with you and be creative about how you might match this in a way others can't.
- Be where your clients are – don't make them come to you; get to them wherever they are right now. Cosy up with a competitor/ partner if that's the way to get access.

You don't have to be niche. They say, "Get niche, get big or get out". I don't say that. I say we all need to back one or more horses in races we think we can win.

Why bother? Why not just tell a good story?

It would be great if we could explain what's true about our product or service and how it meets our customers' needs and for that to be enough. Unfortunately, it's not. We need to commit to a market and message over a period of time. Here's why it's worth it.

- Cornering means owning. You're in control and one step ahead. Your point of view is heard first in the market place. You set the agenda.
- Cornering is efficient. You will gain share of voice faster than your budget would normally permit.
- Cornering is profitable. You can charge more and resist price erosion better than competitors.
- It's also the only way to build value into a company. Turnover and profit means little to investors, if it's not demonstrably sustainable.

Map your customer journey

One of the really nice ways to get to grips with your end-to-end customer journey is to map out a Client Eye View with your team. The results can be surprising and really quite revealing.

"You can put lipstick on a pig, but it's still a pig" Barack Obama, 2009

Many businesses make the mistake of looking at their brand from a narrow, visual perspective; their website, their strapline and of course their logo. These can be great for illustrating your personality or even cement your brand promise in the minds of your customers. But unless what you are trying to communicate is expressed consistently across every touch point and by every employee, every day, all you could be left with is a pig with a penchant for cherry red Rimmel.

Just ask BP. A small fortune spent on their 'Flower Petals' logo and 'Beyond Petroleum' strapline to show a deep commitment to a future without fossil-fuels. One exploding oil rig later followed by the worst environmental disaster in US history, their brand image and environmental credibility is in tatters. Back to the drawing board then (at least for their logo designers).

This is why I plead with business owners to truly understand their end-to-end customer journey. It is this that truly defines your brand; what people see, what people hear, what people experience. And this isn't a 4 stage affair; customer calls, present proposal, deliver product/service, send Invoice. It just doesn't work like that.

Any customer journey is made up of many tens or even hundreds of tiny steps and it pays to understand each and every one of these and identify those 'moments of truth' that make the difference between a happy customer who will come back for more and the unhappy customer who bad mouths you to colleagues (or worse, to the world on Twitter).

To illustrate; why is a neck tie critical to transporting 25 tons of bleach? I spend a fair amount of time on the M4 passing lorries or Logistics Solutions Providers, as they like to be called (always at a legal speed of course). It's amazing how many think they are differentiating themselves through claims of 'Total' or 'Real' logistics solutions, but I don't see any evidence as to how. Just a lazy strapline.

Eddie Stobart, however, get's it. They understand they are not transporting 25 tons of bleach, but have been entrusted with £50,000 of their customers' profit. So how do they articulate (pardon the pun) this promise? Not through a strapline on the trailer but by a driver wearing a uniform and a tie. As a prospective customer, this attention to detail would give me confidence that by showing pride in themselves they will show the same respect for my goods.

One of the really nice ways to get to grips with your end to end customer journey is to map out a Client Eye View with your team. The results can be surprising and really quite revealing. The first step is to forget what you think you know and then literally step into your customer shoes. Be the customer.

Some things to think about;

- **Can they find you in the first place?** Put your product or brand name into Google. Disappointed with the result? Look at how your website is optimised for search and consider investing in Adwords.

- **What are they looking for right now?** Are they browsing, looking for an emerging product or service? Can you deliver this today or is it something you don't have? Sony famously don't conduct customer surveys because they provide products people don't even know they want yet. Kodak had to change their entire business model because they underestimated the impact of digital photography on film sales.

- **Look at the data you already have;** conversion rates from pitch to sale, competitor activity, complaints, customer segment profiles, website visits (length of stay and frequently visited pages).

- **Add richness of insight** – understand how they feel, for example; spend a morning doing a blog scan; what are people saying about you?

- **Qualify what you know** - map out your customer journey step by step and get your customers to rate the things that drive satisfaction and dissatisfaction and how you perform in these areas. You should end up with a line that looks like a heart beat with ups and hopefully not too many downs.

- **Ask yourself; is my money being spent disproportionately in these areas?** Am I focussing resources on areas that I score well in but aren't particularly important to the customer.

- **Look beyond the obvious for that moment of truth.** In the restaurant business it's about getting the toilets right. Swedish petrol company, Preen, used this same insight to target the untapped female driver segment with great success.

- **An idea –** Turn the demand for money process into a warm, feel good moment. Use the back of your invoices to feature a feedback questionnaire. A small and simple solution. As so often these things are.

- **Pick up the phone or log on and test the process.** How does your customer service team greet you, do they have the knowledge to hand? Request a consultation or a quote; did you get an automated reply or a personal call, and which one made you feel more valued?

- **Follow Me Home – not literally of course.** This can be very effective when you have a physical product by looking at how they unpack, install, use and store your product.

- **Use technology to make life easier –** remember when GPS tracking was something you only saw in the movies? Now you can watch parcels making their way across Europe with a couple of mouse clicks. We live in a society of instant gratification and anything that can give your customers real time feedback is valuable.

- **Be prepared to make some tough decisions –** this could be a more ruthless focus on high value customer segments to streamlining your product offering.

The machine

The lead generation machine – a 4x4 approach

Introducing... the Onefish Twofish lead generation machine. We call it the 4x4 approach because it breaks the year into four quarterly cycles and four customer journey steps. Each quarter is focused on one burning industry issue or unmet need, allowing you to showcase a range of highly relevant knowledge and expertise over time.

At its heart, the 4x4 approach is designed to be:

Really, really efficient

Bringing together a number of marketing activities can be incredibly time-consuming, particularly – and we'll talk about it in much more detail later – as great content is at the heart of most campaigns. Producing this content and creating great communication is a heavyweight activity. That's why the lead generation machine limits the amount of brand new content produced, and ensures it is recycled in every possible format. Just like the planet's resources, our own time and budget are finite. Reduce, Reuse, Recycle applies as emphatically to marketing content as it does to household waste.

Manageable and consistent

The big killer of marketing ROI is constant reinvention of the wheel. As marketers, we plan something, start to roll it out and then there's a U-turn to focus on something else. The thinking and set up process begins all over again and the value from the original plan is never derived. This might not happen to all your campaigns, but I would stake a fair wager that this happens at least some of the time. Often an unfocused director is at the heart of these rapid changes in direction. Sometimes the market overtakes us with a new challenge we have to respond to.

The lead generation machine is designed to end this vicious circle in two ways:

- Roughly the same activities happen each quarter. The operation of these becomes habitual and easy to plan and execute. Projects are not starting for the first time, every time, and instead are 'handle turners'. It's easy to build in new elements as new tools and techniques arrive as the existing process is highly automated.
- The quarterly cycle of themes means you can be super-flexible with individual campaigns. Your pipeline of themes can be switched around and new themes dropped in at short notice or zoomed up the priority list if needed, without bringing the existing programme to a standstill.

Measurable and quick to generate a return

I've never been a fan of marketing campaigns which cost the earth to set up and then have little chance of paying back (or at least showing clear signs of success or failure within 6 months). Yes, great campaigns cost money. But many companies have a legacy of expensive, unsuccessful campaigns they would rather forget. To suggest risking adding another one to this list seems quite naïve. So instead, the lead generation machine is designed to produce leading indicators nice and quickly. As a cycle, it should be reviewed and refined every single quarter and the measurables make this possible and desirable.

The new B2B psychological contract

There is a fast emerging psychological contract, largely born out of the web, which we B2B marketers need to understand and work to if we are to be successful.

In a nutshell it goes like this. As marketers we're trying to enter into a dialogue with potential clients in order to get on their radar and start to build a relationship (whether online or real). We want permission to communicate with them and for them to officially enter our lead generation machine.

Prospects are happy to enter into a lead generation machine with a potential provider/partner/vendor provided there is a clear value exchange in which:

- They receive more value than they have to give.
- They are firmly in the driving seat (they call the shots and say when and how they are contacted).
- They feel the value exchange is not sales-led.
- The company is trustworthy in their opinion.

The various types of 'bait' we use to attract prospects and make invisible prospects visible (and therefore contactable) are pretty well understood by business buyers now. We know that if we sign up for a free webinar, we are entering the vendor company's lead generation machine – and if we're lucky we can stay in control of what they send us.

Consider online sign up forms to access restricted content. These are the ultimate value exchange test. At a fixed point in time, prospects can make a choice about whether they are happy with the value exchange or not. The decision is binary – either they sign up, or they don't. Either the content is worth entering the company's lead generation machine for, or it's not.

Once we understand the value exchange, we can start to manipulate it – adding value into the prospect's end and taking away the risk and cost to them at the other.

Value exchanges where the psychological contract applies:

- Online registration to access premium content
- Completion of a web questionnaire to access survey results
- Email sign up to a seminar or webinar
- Agreement to be interviewed for white paper research

Creating the most attractive value exchange possible

Adding in value

- Make the content or event super-specific. We trust and value things that are very focused on our own issues far more than generic offers and we're unlikely to let them slip by.
- Sell what's behind the door – describe the content in terms of benefits to the prospect, use testimonials, find stats or figures to substantiate your claims.
- Use great titling to command attention. Make it specific and outcome focused e.g. "White paper: 10 steps to an industry-leading website which generates 100 leads a month" rather than "White Paper: SEO optimisation".
- Show the price it would be, if you were charging for it.
- Show images or any other kind of tangible evidence.
- Add a bonus item into the pot, e.g. a free white paper if prospects sign up for a webinar.

Taking away risk and cost (both time and money)

- Make it free, or as low cost as you can manage.
- Lower the barrier to entry as much as possible, minimising clicks to click, fields to complete, emails to receive and respond to.
- Make it self service so that people can book in or sign up and access the outcome immediately.
- Have a 'what we do with your data' statement – and make it light, if appropriate (not the standard 'official line' which is barely believable these days).
- Show your company credentials clearly and openly.
- Don't ask the prospect to provide information that is clearly only for your own sales agenda – nothing sends prospects clicking in the opposite direction faster....

The new B2B language rules

Words are hugely important. We make our mind up very rapidly based on the words we read (and of course the visual content they sit within). And because we can all write, we are particularly critical of words that don't resonate with us.

We're looking for:

- relevance (are my keywords in here – the phrases I use to describe projects, issues and interest areas that are pertinent to me right now?)
- difference (are these words 'same old same old' or is there something I haven't heard before?)
- outcome focus (what's in it for me? what can I get for free here? what will save me or make me money? is there an idea here that will make me look clever in front of my boss or team?)
- credibility (are these words telling me a story of competence and trustworthiness?)
- direct (I haven't got time – just tell me straight)
- simple (give me good old Anglo-Saxon words every time)

Meeting all these criteria is a tall order. Add in the challenge of making your words keyword-rich and search engine friendly and it can feel like an unsolvable puzzle. If you've ever wrestled with a positioning or 'what we do' statement, you'll know exactly what I mean.

The challenge is that we are often fishing from a very small stock of words. These words become hackneyed rapidly. Think 'solutions', 'innovative', 'cutting-edge', 'market-leading', 'global player' – all must have been powerful 15 years ago. Now they are so last century.

There's no magic fix, but here are some of the techniques we employ to help clients get round the word challenge.

Use Latin-based words sparingly and only when the context requires precision. Words with a Latin root are longer and more complex than their Anglo Saxon cousins (e.g. 'he articulated' rather than 'he said'). They can sometimes convey arrogance over intelligence. They are hard to read. They take up more space. Write simply and only use the longer Latin words where they are absolutely essential.

Avoid the hackney-pack if you possibly can. Through overuse many words now switch prospects straight off (or best-case scenario, trigger the thought: "Ah, yet another ABC provider"). Solutions, Enhanced, Innovative, Best-in-class, Performance Improvement, Value-add, World-class, Leading-edge, Cutting-edge, Industry-leading, focused on ROI, Results-focused, Core competency, Next generation, Tailored, Bespoke, Extensive experience, Passionate... the list goes on. Not a single one of these words says anything specific about your organisation that will impress a prospect. If you find yourself reaching for a hackney-pack word, you need to look for another (or a different way of phrasing your message).

Consider creating your own phrase that your company can own. We're all driven by keywords and we search for and recognise key phrases that the industry has coined. Cloud computing, SOX and Generation Y are all good examples of phrases that marketers in each respective sector should be tapping into. The only problem is that these phrases become over-used and over-marketed. Sometimes they approximate rather than accurately describe the market we're in.

There is a case for creating our own phrases that we can use to corner our very own markets. If these become well known and are well protected by our lawyers, they can provide huge brand value. We talked about owning our specific market place earlier – inventing and naming one is the ultimate way to do this.

The new look and feel rules

How your brand looks, tastes, sounds and feels matters. You don't need me to tell you that. What might be new to you are the rules that govern prospect expectations in this area. They're important and they're changing.

Prospects are looking for short cuts to understanding how credible and suitable you are for them. They will decode and deconstruct your brand unconsciously using their industry frames of reference. Here's where we're at right now and what you should be considering.

Rule 1: Be in the race

Absolute, top-of-the-list, must have – does your brand's look and feel make you a credible player or not? If not, you're out of the race before you've even started. When potential clients come to me with a lead generation campaign that's not working for them, the first thing I do is check out their brand. What's the first thing we do, if we receive a call or email suggesting a meeting? If we're even half way interested, we take a look at their website. If it's a shambles, we're out of there. It's a nice shortcut we use every day to filter out companies we're definitely not interested in. Don't fall at the first hurdle.

What they're expecting

- Brand identity: in line with 66% of the market (i.e. no more than one step away from two thirds of the brands they will be used to seeing), contemporary and at least halfway modern.
- Website: should look like you've spent some money on it. Obviously templated sites are out, clutter is dangerous, homemade sites (or graphic additions made yourself via a content management system) spell disaster.

Rule 2: Get your story straight

Prospects want to feel that you're clearly committed to their market, not hedging your bets on a number of different horses. Focus is power – we've established that already. Your look and feel should express that very clearly.

What they're expecting

- Brand identity: very consistent application of your brand throughout every medium, series and sets i.e. products and services grouped into identifiable 'lines' and visually coded accordingly.
- Website: Very clear hierarchy of information on the site, logical information architecture and navigation, clear positioning statement up front on the homepage, specificity of proposition, breadcrumb trail to make navigation super-easy.

Rule 3: The right gender

Yes indeed, corporate identity or look and feel is gendered. I see a great deal of masculinised and feminised branding and collateral. That's not to say that men always create one kind of brand and women another – it's just a way to describe two opposing ends of a communication style spectrum. What's needed is a unisex approach that brings the best of both sexes together and works with your core audience.

Masculine communication is:

- direct, factual
- outcome focused
- short, though sometimes cluttered
- all about the numbers and the process
- primary colours or monotone.

Feminine communication is:

- story or analogy based
- long or wordy
- clearly signposted
- indirect or implicit
- all about the relationship and the feel-good factor
- softer colours, softer imagery.

Clearly style and tone will depend greatly on your market, niche and audience — but the following rules will stand you in good stead whatever your market.

- Be direct and succinct — but use stories to illustrate.
- No clutter (ever, ever, ever).
- Balance ROI and relationship focused messages — both are important.
- Deliver personality — but never be cute.
- Be explicit.
- Steer clear of very soft or very hard brand designs, no matter what your marketplace.

Getting your machine set up

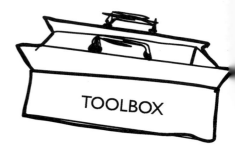

TOOLBOX

Before you get your machine up and running, you'll need some kit to run it on. These are all the things you should have set up and in place.

Key message guide

We always insist on getting this set of messages clear, upfront in any kind of lead generation or content-related project. It's purely an internal document so it doesn't need to be wordsmithed but it does need to reflect the language you use to talk about your business.

It's a one page grid that sums up everything a marketer or agency might need to know to produce a campaign idea that's 80% right first time. It's also a document that the management team (or whoever signs the marketing budget) should sign off. They don't need to worry about finesse or words, but they DO need to endorse the overall framework. This gives you great scope for having 'on brief/off brief' conversations both internally and with agencies.

Here's the grid – and I've populated it with our own key messages so that you see how it might work in practice.

Audience - organisation

- Complex B2B sale – consultancy, technology, professional services
- Serious growth agenda – possibly building for sale or exit
- £1m - £100m turnover
- UK South East and Central Europe

Audience – individual buyers

- Growth-focused CEOs and MDs
- Innovative marketers
- Individuals who feel:
  - We're not getting traction fast enough
  - We're wasting money on too many different activities
  - Our internal approach/team isn't working
  - We know we sell and deliver great work – we just need to meet more people

SINGLE UNEQUIVOCAL PROPOSITION:
- We enable our clients to generate large or complex deals in big companies, through a strategic, creative, super-efficient marketing methodology for B2Bs.

Key messages

- We help businesses sell complex or IP-based services to big companies, working with around 50 fast growth companies every year
- We're an end-to-end B2B marketing agency – from strategy to execution, including research, creative, copy, digital and film
- We're experts in 'strategic creativity' – helping organisations become the standout player in their market place
- We're easy to work with, strategic, creative and full of energy

Unmet needs we're tapping into

- Shortage of hires/agencies who can understand the complex product or service AND create a campaign pitched at the right level of sophistication AND manage the detail of an integrated marketing campaign
- Tight budget but big agenda – needs to be ruthlessly effective without a 'big company' budget
- Loads of ideas for tapping into market potential but no time to execute them internally

DID YOU HEAR THE ONE ABOUT THE BUSINESS?

You might also consider using this grid for individual product or service campaigns. It's a great way to get clear about the shape and size of a target market and define the parameters of a lead generation activity.

One-liner about your business

If you don't already have one of these (or if you have one but no one agrees on it) it's time to nail this down. Be clear that it won't be a permanent fixture – but it must exist, even if it's updated in the medium term. Otherwise, there is no consistent banner under which to hang your lead generation machine.

This is not a strapline. It's a very short elevator pitch. It's the line that should sit on the front page of your website and in your email signatures. It's the line that puts your core competence firmly into the context of your market's unmet needs and the industry you're in.

It might comprise two lines: a headline and a sub-line.

Virtrium is a very successful IT consultancy. Here is an example of two alternative one-liners they considered with our help.

First version – with a headline and subline

Running IT as a business:

Service Delivery and Sourcing to streamline IT as a commercial operation

Second version – a straight elevator statement

Virtrium helps IT deliver savings, make powerful investments and commercialise the function, with a particular focus on recession-bitten sectors like Financial Services and Retail.

I'll let you mull over which version they went with in the end!

And here's ours:

We help businesses sell clever things to other companies (with a focus on complex or IP-based sales like consultancy, technology and professional services).

Your challenge is to pitch your one-liner at the right level. Too specific and you'll narrow down the market and exclude future service development. Too vague and you'll instantly become a me-too. Hopefully the examples above give you some ideas on how to strike the right balance.

Boilerplate text

Following on rapidly from your one-liner is a set of boilerplate text – essentially a longer, fuller version of your 1-liner. This text is used at the bottom of your press releases, case studies and collateral. If a journalist or an event organiser asks for this, you can fire it straight over. It's actually quite factual as it's a context setter – the sexier creative copy is a variation on this and would be much more creative and probably shorter too.

This is your 'default copy' where a sexy approach is not needed but something very clear and very signed off is needed quickly.

Once you get your boilerplate text organised, you'll be surprised how useful it becomes and how much time it saves you.

Other boilerplates you might find it useful to create:
- Speaker or director biographies (one to two paragraphs for press releases plus a full version of around 400 words)
- Product or service boilerplates (if you are running campaigns around particular service areas, you'll find this pretty much essential)

'What we do' PDFs

Once you've packaged up what you do, it can be immensely helpful to have some clear PDFs that you can email to potential clients along with case studies or knowledge articles. On their own, they are not marketing tools, they're sales tools. When they sit in the context of the Lead Generation Machine, they make the connection between engaged prospects and prospects asking to buy something. So they are important.

Prospects are looking for some very specific things from a one-pager and we need to orient the content precisely around the way their mind is working.

Here are the questions at the tip of their tongue:
- What does this company do overall? (They're trying to decode you and put you in a pigeonhole. To a certain extent, you have to help them do this, otherwise you're too complicated to process, mentally, or you risk them popping you in entirely the wrong box....)
- Do they understand my needs, my industry and where I am? (Or are they just trying to push product at me?)
- What can I buy and what difference will it make to me in clear, simple terms I can believe? (They want to see 'what it is' and 'what you get out of it' in the same breath)
- How does it work? (You may need more or less in this area, depending on how well established your product or service area is, but with complex or IP-based sales often a short guide to the 'how' goes a long way to proving your credibility)
- What's the scale? Are there options? (Is this something for companies much bigger or much smaller than my own or are there different levels at which I can get access to the promised results?)
- Who else uses this? How credible is it? What do my peers think?
- What can I do next? (Ideally, prospects want both a self service route e.g. a further download or web link *plus* a direct contact route. Give them both choices wherever possible.)

Big health warning! We need to take a HUGE step away from the traditional 'data sheet' approach, favoured by so many technology companies.

Old school data sheets

- Product, service and specification led
- Oriented around 'what we sell'
- Visually dull and boring
- Passive – expect prospects to make contact

'What we do' PDFs

- Context and need led
- Oriented around 'the value you can buy'
- Visually laid out to tell a story
- Proactive – provide prospects with a path they can join you on

Strong, clear website

Gosh, so much to say, so little space! This is a huge, huge area and one I can't hope to tackle in a short section. But I think we can set some clear guidelines at a high level that you can use to develop a strong clear website.

First let's be clear about the purpose of the website. This is my priority order for my own company website. You might find it helpful to create your own website priority objective list from which you can create your web strategy and measure back.

My website is on this planet to:

- provide an online home and a source of instant credibility for my company
- turn the buzz we create around Onefish Twofish into visible prospects with whom we can start a conversation
- enable people (looking to buy what we sell) to find us

If we take these criteria, one-by-one, we come up with something like this:

Objective	High level principles for the site
Online home and credibility	The homepage must provide the perfect entry point for visitors who may have come directly to it, or alternatively may have 'deep-landed' on a content page and helicoptered up to the home page to see what it's all about.

This means:

- your one-line statement clearly at the top of the hierarchy so that visitors can see your overall context immediately
- very clear, logical signposting of content – you absolutely can't use the homepage as a merry-go-round for new offerings, concepts or events/activities, unless they are well structured within the overall layout (e.g. a section called 'This month's key industry issue')
- your creative Big Idea clearly expressed on the homepage – not another set of imagery or creative that happens to be there
- critical entry points to important content which are updated regularly
- some kind of client or other third party endorsement, right there on the homepage
- very obvious contact details – even if no one picks up the phone, huge trust is built by knowing that they can

The rest of the site must build on this credibility in more detail, specifically:

- Case studies and tangible examples of work - these help to indicate scale, which is very important. If we don't understand the scale of the proposition we're looking at (i.e. whether it's a big company or a small company solution, or an end-to-end or a lightweight solution) we switch off very quickly. Case studies provide visitors with a benchmark against which they can measure themselves.
- Testimonials and third party endorsement.
- Regularly updated, high value content (we'll talk about this in MUCH more detail later).
- Collation of industry information – if you can be a hub and filter for great content from throughout the industry you'll go far.
- Personality and culture – whatever your brand, your website should reflect it in language, imagery and navigation. Dry, listless websites will never build credibility.
- A strong 'about us' section which includes people profiles and a background to the history and philosophy of the company. Missing this piece out harms credibility instantly and poses the question "What's NOT being said and why?"

Some bonus ideas to consider from truly credibility-building websites

- Is there a statistic you can claim ownership of, e.g. "Eight of the 10 global banks trust us to..." or "96% of our clients would recommend us to their peergroup"?
- Can you show what you do visually (not a cheesy, top level, consultancy-style schematic but something that truly helps people understand more about their own problem and what they can do about it)?
- Can you help buyers with their early stage research? If you sell a product, Buyers' Guides are invaluable. If you sell a service, "Looking for XYZ: Your Options" guides are also great, provided they are not heavily biased towards your solution.

Turn buzz into leads

This is huge. A big part of the Lead Generation Machine is to build a head of steam around your website via the wonderful range of social media options available to us. Without a clear plan, the risk is that your website traffic climbs, but most of these people remain invisible to you. Therefore you can't identify them or build a relationship with them.

Here's how to make sure that you're making as many of the invisible people, visible, as possible.

- Make sure you have a restricted content area on your website, accessible only through a simple login. Put the best 25% of your content behind this login, so that most of your information is freely available to sample, but the really good stuff requires a registration.
- Create accessibility – make it super-easy to register for content (no complicated double login system where you have to jump through hoops and then go back in to a find the piece of content you originally wanted). Make it short and simple and sell the simplicity with clear signposting e.g. "You're a click away from…" or "Step 1 of 2". We have a Small Business Marketing Ideabook which we flag as follows: Download the Small Business Marketing Ideabook (you'll need to register, but it's free and only takes a jiffy).
- Sell that content. Choose a specific, keyword rich, high impact title and provide a landing page that sells the content clearly and thoroughly.

Here's the copy from the Small Business Marketing Ideabook landing page:

"Onefish Twofish is all about generating lots more opportunities and sales for businesses selling to other businesses. We've pulled together all our best marketing ideas into one bumper ideabook!

Our work with some of the fastest growing consultancies and service providers has enabled us to innovate left, right and centre, with remarkable results. For the first time we spill the beans...

Download the ideabook for:

- the pyramid approach - how to dramatically improve conversion
- what really drives B2B purchasing decisions - and how to tap into it
- the complete 62-point B2B event checklist
- the secret to opening new relationships without selling
- 9 ways to improve your proposal success rate
- a complete how to guide for getting the best out of Google adwords, email newsletters, advertising and cold pitching

Registered and logged in already?

(**DOWNLOAD IDEABOOK**)

Other good ways to make invisible visitors, visible.

Invite visitors to be part of your next research project: everyone likes to be an opinion-former. Describe the industry insight you are researching (more about this in Step One of the Machine) and invite visitors to submit themselves as expert interviewees.

Enable sign up to your industry leading newsletter (although it won't be called a newsletter – see Step Four of the Machine!): showcase previous newsletters and provide options for sign up throughout the site.

Deploy a 'request a proposal' form: if you don't already have one (perhaps because what you sell is way too clever and complex), consider a button on every page which takes visitors to a form they can complete with a very brief outline of their problem, required outcome and possible budget. This is a really nice way to manage potential tyre-kickers as you're asking them to do some of the up front qualification and avoiding endless qualifying phone calls.

Use out of the ordinary contact forms: we all have a contact form (or at least we should have) but there are two nice ways to optimise these even further for those who really do want to get in touch.

Have a 'Request a Call Back' form in the side bar or masthead of every page. The form should be on the page itself so that visitors can pop their details straight in and submit. This makes the simplicity of the form explicit and dramatically increases the completion rate.

Pump your current form with personality and value. Rather than "Use the form below to contact us with a query" (the ultimate in yawn-inducing form copy), trying something that suggests value lies on the other side of the submit button, like...

- "Tell us your biggest challenge and the budget you'd be willing to part with to solve it completely and we'll send you a roadmap and cost breakdown within 3 working days."
- "Need to think aloud about something? Book some informal telephone time with a Client Director."

And finally, consider a Web Visitor Visibility tool, like Prospectvision: site visitors leave a trail. Web visitor visibility tools attempt to decode this trail and tell you who has visited your site, *even* if they haven't registered their details or completed a form. It's done through the visitor's IP address and the outcome is a list of all the companies the tool can identify (including company name, web address and country) and their activity on the site (where they went, how long they spent on the site etc). It's the back door route, but it can be incredibly effective in revealing who is searching for your services, based on buzz you have generated around your site.

Enable prospects to find us
This part is all about search engine optimisation AND being linked from the right places.

If organisations are searching for a company providing our services, we want to be easy to find and clearly referenced in the places they are looking, Google being the really obvious one.

If this is huge for you, please do skip straight to the section about search engine marketing a little later on where there's a more thorough discussion.

In the meantime, here are some principles to be getting your head around, if you want to make it easier for people to find you.

Be visible on Google – get a proper Google search engine strategy going for keywords your potential clients are searching on. There are far too many great businesses which are basically invisible on Google. We cover how to do this later in the book. The point I'm making now is that this is a non-negotiable, even if you assure me that decision makers are not searching for potential providers on the web. This is almost never true. We all use Google all the time, even if we're not actually searching for "Potential New Partner I've Never Heard Of For Large Consultancy Project". It's part of the fabric of doing business and you need to be present.

Be listed in the right directories – whether this is an industry resource website, a governing body or industry institute, a vendor/partner review list or an event directory. If you're not there, you can't be found. If you're there, you just might be found and it might be the final piece in the jigsaw that prompts a potential client to give you a call.

Be good at sweating your online presence – whatever events you run or content you produce, sweat them in every possible online space. Sites which won't promote your company will promote your events and content so use these as levers to get as many links back to your site as possible. You'll find the effect is far wider/ greater than just event sign ups or content downloads.

A proposal template

Depending on what and how you sell, you'll probably use one or more of the following:

- a honking great Word doc based proposal
- a short, dry quote sheet (possibly automatically produced)
- a range of PowerPoint Wonders – decks created and manipulated by sales people and possibly the help of a 'creative PA' to tailor a proposal to a specific client.

All these are de rigeur, but for me, none of them quite hit the spot and potentially all are either too time-consuming or too low impact to hit the mark.

My suggestion is that you take a look at the way you write proposals and either overhaul the whole approach... or just take some tips from my quick win suggestions.

Less like the FT and more like Grazia

Proposals typically start as Microsoft Word documents, in A4 portrait format, with lots of closely packed text, stretching right across the page. To me, this is the way they are easiest to create, not the way they are easiest and most impactful to read.

Like any other document, we scan rather than read. So let's take lessons from high-selling magazines like Grazia (arguably the most successful new entrant into the very competitive women's category in the last few years).

Here's what magazines like Grazia do really well

- Signposting: you know exactly where you are in the publication, all the way through. This makes it easy to dip in and out of, rather than having to follow the linear, chronological pattern from start to finish.

- Layout: multi-column formats are used throughout and readers never get bogged down trying to read right across the page.

- Bitesize chunks: the content is broken up into manageable pieces which are easy to scan and read.

- Headers that tell the story: rather than using generic headings (e.g. 'your challenge', 'our solution') which are clear but have zero other value, use the header copy to lift your expertise off the page.

- Visuals and graphics: images, screenshots and schematics all help bring a proposal to life, break up the text and feed people who digest visuals better than words.

Do: create mood boards of imagery to trigger ideas, take screen shots of previous work you've done (even reports in Word can work well), create simple schematics, tabulate information (e.g. before and after, or 'what we do' and 'what you'll get').

Don't: put cheesy stock imagery with hard edges onto each slide – very retro these days and screams 'how can I make this page more interesting?!'

1, 2, 3, 200, 10,000000!

Numbers

When I was media trained, I was taught that numbers are the sizzle that sells. I've since tried to put them into everything I can – provided they are credible, that is.

Ideas for using numbers:

- Does your service mean something changes/reduces/increases by an average percentage per client?

- Can you point to a large number of clients/countries/languages/end users/projects?

- Is there a proportion of a specific market you can claim e.g. 50% of the FTSE250 use some part of your product or service?

- Can you translate a client saving or gain into something tangible (e.g. 'our clients report time savings of 6 weeks per user per year – that's £88,000 per year in salary savings for an average firm')?

- Can you create a mini-ROI calc (ideally where they can play around with the assumptions and base numbers) that will spit out some interesting pay back stats?

- Try the old 'decreasing numbers' trick e.g. '1,800 consultants, 146 FTSE 250 clients, 40 languages, 23 countries, 1 sought after law firm'.

- Or 'Your Company In Numbers' e.g.

Onefish Twofish in numbers:

- 15 expert B2B marketers
- 50 fast track clients working closely with us
- 1 million+ market touchpoints on behalf of our clients in 2009
- 17.4% average client revenue growth in 2009/10

"IT IS A BIT EMBARRASSING
TO HAVE BEEN CONCERNED WITH THE
HUMAN PROBLEM ALL ONE'S LIFE
AND FIND AT THE END THAT ONE HAS NO
MORE TO OFFER BY WAY OF ADVICE THAN
"TRY TO BE A LITTLE KINDER""

Aldous Huxley

Quotes: I like to use quotes in proposals – but not just testimonials (which are awfully salesy, after all). I grab insight statements from clients which are actually helpful in their own right, not just credibility-building for us. Then I put them in a clear box, wrap the rest of the text around them and voila – there's a useful, credible quote which is valuable to the reader and implicitly endorses us.

Another idea to consider: external quotes, insights and stats. You could open each section with a pithy quote from a guru, or pinch some external stats which back up your proposed solution.

Trying a new format

If you're feeling like overhauling your proposal format altogether, I can highly recommend it for shaking things up and getting sales moving again (particularly if you're getting stuck at pitching stage).

Here are a few ideas to consider:

- Switch from portrait to landscape and a 2 or 3 column format. This is instantly more dynamic (although you'll need good skills in Word to use this efficiently). Use the first 1 or 2 columns for the main content and the right hand column for quotes, stats, ideas, imagery etc.

- Put a one-page summary at the very start which includes everything and therefore is a true exec summary:
    - What you've asked for help with
    - What we recommend
    - The outcomes you can expect (and the risks if you do nothing)
    - Options we think you should consider
    - The estimated cost (yes, I really do want you to put the cost right at the front! It shows confidence and gets straight to the heart of the matter)

- Get an agency to create you a truly winning format which you can use and customise internally. Be brave and take on their suggestions – they just might be able to increase your conversion rate by a couple of clicks.

If you are completely wedded to the more traditional format, we have a really nice version of this on our website (www.onefishtwofish.co.uk -> ideas) which you can steal and customise.

Email signature

Use it, sweat it, flaunt it. Most companies are getting pretty savvy at this, but it's worth checking yours:

- looks clean, consistent and clear and reflects your brand
- includes a one-liner about what you do (the home page positioning statement from your website)
- has some personality
- includes a latest news item and link.

This is my email signature. We all have one like this at Onefish Twofish (and a fun first-day activity for each joiner is to decide what to put in their 'what I do' section). It's right for us but it might not be right for you – that said, I know at least 20 companies who have copied it so there is something nice about the 3 column format which makes good use of the space. It also doesn't use any actual images so slips through spam filters with ease.

Email delivery system

A big part of the Lead Generation Machine is sending emails. Contrary to some people's opinion, email marketing absolutely does work. It's only the bad stuff we call spam and delete with a derisory 'pah!'.

So you need a mechanism for sending emails that is going to work for you and be cost effective. Actually, you need two ways to send emails - this might require two different systems, depending on the vendors you're working with.

Here's a guide to the two types of email you'll need to send and what the advantages and disadvantages of each are likely to be.

Email type 1: Plain text (aka 1:1)

Main purpose: to feel like a personal 1:1 email and generate a 'reply to' response.

How it works: Downloadable software that sits on your machine and sends emails through your own server.

It's like sending a regular email but mail merging it to a bulk list. Online software-as-a-service that is hosted remotely and sends emails through its own server and service provider. You upload the content/imagery and the system puts everything together and sends.

Options: Send straight from your current CRM. Act, Sugar, Salesforce.com and several other mainstream CRMs will have a bulk mail distribution option, the advantage being that the data and tagging remains within your current system (no exporting and importing).

or

Buy a 1:1 email system like WorldMerge or G–Lock 5. I think Outlook might have improved its mail merge facility, but I've never actually used it.

Advantages

- Simple to set up and send
- Feels like a personal email
- More likely to get through spam filters
- More likely to generate a 'reply to' response
- Can be cheaper to send
- May work directly from your existing CRM e.g. Act or Sugar

Disadvantages

- No branding
- Hard to track activity
- Managing lists and sends can be a bit unwieldy
- Limited to the number of sends per day by your Internet Service Provider (usually 1,500 on a normal package)
- Can go under the radar and fail to be noticed

Email type 2: HTML

Main purpose: to build brand awareness, present content in a sleek, shiny format, to promote a product, service or event.

How it works: Online software-as-a-service that is hosted remotely and sends emails through its own server and service provider. You upload the content/imagery and the system puts everything together and sends.

Options: Choose from a wide range of online systems including:
www.dotmailer.com
www.newzapp.co.uk
www.sign-up.to
www.ConstantContact.com
www.CommuniGator.co.uk
www.MailChimp.com
www.CheetahMail.com

We like NewZapp as it's one of the most comprehensive systems, the customer service is excellent, it gets through spam filters like nobody's business and the templating system works really well.

Advantages

- Fully branded up – look and feel is more high impact and memorable
- Can track opens and clicks
- Perfect for newsletters and event invites

Disadvantages

- Feels like advertising (impersonal)
- Usually far less control over the layout and formatting due to templating
- Often need an agency to produce the html
- Recipient can't see the images until you click 'load images'
- Includes the mandatory footer so always feels salesy

Client Relationship Management system

Your Client Relationship Management system (CRM) is the foundation of slick and well-managed marketing. No system does everything so you'll always need to compromise. But here's what your system should (ideally) do.

- Categorise companies and contacts in a relational database.
- Manage opportunities and pipeline (so you can track marketing activity through the value chain).
- Segment and tag the list into clear email/mailing lists e.g. Christmas party, research invite, newsletter, all Capital Markets firms with a European HQ (or whatever the criteria might be).
- Flag and track opportunity sources, so we know what happens to people who have (for example) requested a research paper.
- Assign specific ownership, clearly showing who is responsible for developing business with each contact and what has happened to each of these leads.
- Tag who you're selling what to, so that you can identify cross selling opportunities and campaigns based on purchase history.
- Calculate conversion scores by client, service area, sales person and org type.
- Send bulk email (in a perfect world – otherwise, you can export and use another system each time).

Companies and contacts should be tagged separately.

You can download a spreadsheet guide to best practice tagging on the Onefish Twofish website (www.onefishtwofish.co.uk -> ideas), if you'd like some help getting off a blank piece of paper.

An Advisory Board

An idea to consider… could an advisory board build credibility and momentum into your machine?

When being a heavyweight is a must, there are few better tactics than gathering a group of clever, experienced people around your business in the form of an advisory board.

What's the big idea?

The idea is to host regular meetings and invite a panel of Important People from your sector (or beyond) to attend. In terms of organisation, this is pretty simple. A meeting room or private room in a restaurant is all that is required. And there's no need to make a huge presentation as it's their opinions that count, not yours.

Is it worth the effort?

When measured against the relatively modest costs, the rewards are fantastic. You get:

- real feedback on the issues in your industry and your business's offering and/or new service ideas
- ideas and innovative thinking about the future and diverse discussions (make sure you invite loud people from very different parts of the sector e.g. in house experts and academics)
- the opportunity to leverage the profile of those in your advisory board on your website, in proposals, in conversation
- an event to which existing prospects/clients can be invited as guests
- strong relationships with opinion leaders
- a reason to contact important, but hard to reach prospects
- content for research papers, sector updates and other insight-led marketing communications
- prospective fodder for journalists and PR opportunities (using this content).

Ok, I get it. How do I get started?

Glad you're on board with the idea. We agree - it's a gem. Here's what to do.

1. Decide on some objectives for your board. Are you looking for deep industry feedback or is it really about potential referrals? This will determine who you invite.

2. Make a list of potential members. Ten will be fine to start off with. Choose a wide range of people - existing clients, potential clients, journalists, academics, opinion leaders, partner organisations, end users, competitors (why not?!), entrepreneurs etc.

3. Choose a name for your board. You could argue this is optional, but here at Onefish Twofish we like things to have a good name – we think it really brings things together.

4. Set a date and a venue. Lunch in the private room of a restaurant is fine.

5. Invite people! Four to six is the ideal actual group size for the meetings (excluding people from your business) so you'll need to invite at least ten in the first instance as some will turn

down your kind offer and some will join the board but be unable to make the date.

6. Invite more, if needed. If you're not sure whether someone will make a good board member, invite them as a guest the first time. You can ask them to join as a permanent member later if you like them and they are a good fit.

7. Host your event. A bit of structure is good e.g. some core questions to cover. Be prepared to deviate on the day. Don't try to cover too much.

8. Get some feedback about what the members would like to get out of it. Draw up some (short) guidelines so they know what the deal is - what's expected of them, what they'll get in return, how they can leave the advisory board etc.

9. Leverage the event: Publish a news item on your website. Write a summary of the insight gained for your newsletter. Add the board to your 'about us' section on your website (including bios and photos). Add some text about the board and its members to your proposal templates.

10. Run another event - you get the idea...

PART 2:
Running your machine

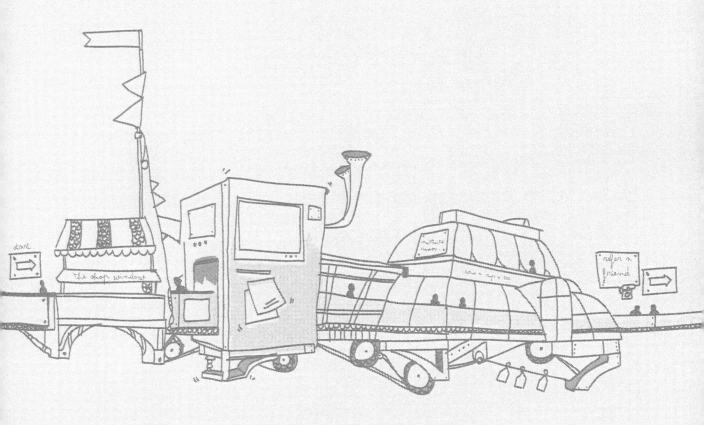

You've built your foundation. Your website is buzzing. Your boilerplate text is proofed. You're ready to pull the cord on your machine. Let's get started.

Step One:
Create great content

(take ownership of the market place)

First things first. The Lead Generation Machine is designed around owning a market place. Having successfully identified your target market (the piece – or pieces - of ground that you can own and position yourself firmly in) and built the foundations, the first step of actually running your machine is to claim ownership of this market by expressing your knowledge and expertise through exceptional content. Content (articles, white papers, film, webinars, seminars, online diagnostic tools, ideabooks) is the currency of lead generation in the B2B environment.

It's what potential clients are willing to give up their privacy for.

It asserts our authority in the market place and allows us to make a big noise, without hacking everyone off with sales messages.

It allows us to express our organisation's opinion.

It positions us in the right space and at the right price point.

It answers the prospect's questions at every stage of the buying cycle.

The key challenge is producing content that holds its own with intelligent buyers, BUT doesn't require your most expensive people to take ten weeks away from selling/billing to create.

In practice, this means we need to be smart about what and how much we create. Otherwise, we'll grind to a halt trying to produce the most high impact content and having to settle for far less when this proves impossible.

What is Super Content and how much is enough?

I talk about Super Content when I mean the 'must-read' content in a particular space. It's the article/ebook/webfilm/tool that everyone has a copy of because it's so great. It's tried, tested and trusted. It contains either:

- an amazing piece of insight that breaks new ground (this is thought leadership)

or

- a fantastically practical guide to something organisations really need to do/think about/respond to (this is opinion leadership).

With one eye on the clock and the budget, my experience tells me that one fantastic piece of content each quarter (per main target market – and you may only have one) is usually enough to drive all the sales and marketing you need. If you can't produce something great in three months, you're probably in the wrong game.

You could produce more items if you wanted to and had the inclination and time – for example CEOs who blog prolifically and happily will churn out far more than one great piece of content each quarter to your company's great benefit. But focus and quality over quantity are my mantras.

What does Super Content look like?

Competition for content is high – but you only need to be one step better than your competitors. If you search for articles in your marketplace, you may well find a surfeit of low-to-moderate quality content. These tend to be produced as search engine fodder, full of keywords and strewn across the online market place. Another glance will reveal the great work of professional publishing houses, for example Harvard Business Review (oft lauded as the ultimate Super Content!). If you look even more closely, you might find a few gems created by competitors – real Super Content, created and delivered expertly.

We're ideally trying to emulate the publishing houses to produce something exceptional – but under our own guise. No easy task.

Here are some nice examples of titles which have 'sold' well online.

"100 ways to grow your consulting firm in a recession"
(produced by Equiteq and a great read)

"Talent strategy for *real* business"
(published by Xancam Consulting)

"More time, more money"
(written by Shirlaws Coaching - highly recommended for business owner-managers)

"Soft Skills, Hard Dollars"
(a powerful critique of coaching by GPR Dehler)

"Capitalizing on Complexity"
(insights from the 2010 IBM Global CEO Study)

"Decide and Deliver: Five Steps to Breakthrough Performance in Your Organization"
(the featured Bain publication at the time of going to press)

External research: the backbone of great Super Content

You could just pour insight out of your own heads and into a piece of content (expert bloggers do it all the time, with not inconsiderable success!). But I think this is a missed opportunity. Your marketplace will inherently mistrust your organisation's insight, however well stated and positioned. They will however value and respect:

- the views of their peers
- credible statistics from their market place
- insights from industry thinkers, journalists and business schools
- secondary research conducted by industry bodies.

The Lead Generation Machine advocates creating Super Content based on collecting data and insight externally. In many cases this can actually speed up the content production process because the findings are rich and the insight easy to spell out. We'll talk later about how to design a research method that will work for you.

I've let it slip by almost unnoticed – but the huge and powerful side benefit of collecting external information to create your Super Content is that you get the opportunity to engage the market while you produce content (you don't need to wait until you have shiny copies on your bookshelf to get the value from it). It's a reason to:

- talk to potential clients who might not otherwise take your call
- ask for introductions to new people in existing clients or in your network (what better way to use LinkedIn?!)
- create and foster peer-to-peer relationships with senior people in existing clients.

YOU WIN!

And of course, if you interview them, you get to have a phone call or a face-to-face meeting – a great way to truly get on their radar and win them over with your clever questions.

Given that the Lead Generation Machine is about opening up conversations with the right people in the right organisations, external research with potential clients is an invaluable tool for this.

The win-win-win of good Super Content

Done the right way, Super Content can be a huge win-win-win for your business and your network and it goes straight to the heart of the principles of the Lead Generation Machine (i.e. getting maximum value out of the minimum activity and spend).

- Your target audience gets complimentary access to your research, networking opportunities with their opposite numbers in other organisations and lots of ideas to take with them.
- You get fantastic market insight and a White Paper to attract prospects and press hounds.
- You build new relationships with individuals from your target market who have a specific interest in your area of expertise.

What Super Content options should you be considering?

Content	What it is	Great for
White paper	A research-led report or paper exploring an industry hot question and posing an answer based on primary or secondary research	Showing off your research to companies that want stats and facts
Ebook	A practical, online mini-book (c. 15-50 pages) on a hot topic	Sharing your knowledge without writing an actual book
Book	A regular, hard copy book!	Tangible evidence of your expertise and huge credibility
Web film or webcast	Delivery of opinion or research through video on the web	Bringing your message to life and showcasing your key people
Podcast series	An iTunes (or other media player/ aggregator) series of audio files which potential clients can subscribe and listen to	Building credibility over time and dominating a new media type

How to produce your piece of Super Content each quarter

Choose the right topic

Ideally you should have a pipeline of themes, related directly to the range of propositions you want to introduce and sell into to the marketplace. For some of you, this will be obvious – for example, at Onefish Twofish, our four themes this year follow the four steps of the Lead Generation Machine. For some of you, just defining themes will try to absorb as much of your time as humanly possible. Here's how to choose a good, flexible pipeline without bringing the marketing team to a standstill...

- Start with your propositions – what four to six propositions will drive profitability and growth in the business (hopefully a conversation that has already taken place)?

- What issues can you tie these into (either one issue per proposition or a set of issues explored one-by-one which you can solve in a number of ways)?

- Think about how you can craft these issues so they directly relate to your work (i.e. you're not just researching and discussing a topic that doesn't help people understand what you do and how you can help them) but are not so focused that your Super Content looks like a sales document.

- I like to have a pipeline of four to six topics and a rough idea of the order I will run them in. But I keep things flexible in case new opportunities come up and I add ideas to the mix all the time.

Create a headline-driven approach

This is a really important concept. We could consider ourselves PhD students, looking for the truth, which is surely out there. We might start with a hypothesis but we are looking to prove it empirically. Actually, this is marketing, not science. That's not to say we're inventing figures or twisting the statistics (far from it) but the purpose of the research is completely different. It's closer to journalism in that we're trying to create a story, a message, a reason for people to stop and think – and we're trying to position our own company as the owner of this piece of thinking.

This requires a headline-driven approach. Start with the headlines you would ideally like to see and work backwards. Headlines are best when they are 'Man Bites Dog' style. They point out something that is unexpected and important.

In B2B research, one of my favourite approaches is to juxtapose two contrasting statistics side by side to create a Market Need Gap. Here are a few (exaggerated!) examples of how it might work.

Statistic one: "99% of CEOs agree that a strong pipeline of internal talent is the single biggest factor in their organisation's long term success."

Statistic two: "But only 1% of organisations have a talent strategy in place to deliver a pipeline of future leaders."

Market Need Gap: 98% of organisations need to create a talent strategy

Possible headline: "Blue Chips point to development of a powerful talent strategy as the biggest land-grab opportunity in the war for talent"

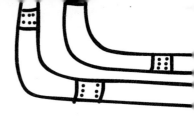

Or try this for size...

Statistic one: "99% of small businesses believe they could grow their business in double figures if they had twice as many opportunities in their pipeline."

Statistic two: "But only 1% of these small businesses have a lead generation strategy."

Market Need Gap: 98% of organisations need a lead generation strategy.

Possible headline: "Double the opportunities in your pipeline with a lead generation strategy"

Or a variation...

Statistic one: "65% of IT projects fail to deliver the value they were originally designed to create."

Statistic two: "Of those that do succeed, 97% have a steering committee which meets and completes agreed actions at least once a month, compared with only 12% in failed projects."

Market Need Gap: Steering committees which meet regularly and complete agreed actions can make the difference between IT project success and failure.

Possible headline: "Steering committee is the key to IT project success"

Important caveat: a single piece of research can only prove a relationship between two variables – it can't prove cause and effect, which can only be done through repeated research over a period of time (longitudinal research). So we're exploring opinions here, not proving determinants of business/project success or failure. Nevertheless, you can see the power of combining statistics in the way I'm describing.

Design your research programme

Once you've decided on the topics and headlines you would ideally like to achieve, it's time to create a research approach that will work for you.

Obviously, there are many, many ways to collect data, but here are the options I usually consider and why.

Interviews

How: telephone or face-to-face interview, using a semi-structured interview guide.

Who with: decision makers in potential clients (you won't do many so the quality should be high).

Best for: building personal relationships, getting introduced, gathering qualitative, detailed insight, getting quotes from credible industry players.

Web survey

How: create a web survey using a low-cost survey tool and distribute across the marketplace.

Who with: all potential clients, contacts at every level.

Best for: producing cold, hard statistics, generating a large number of leads (accepting that the quality might be variable), creating a very credible and possibly statistically significant dataset that the press will pick up.

Desk research

How: use the internet to find previous research projects, quotes, books or sets of data which relate to your topic.

Best for: third party credibility, padding out a research project with a thin response, presenting a more well-rounded, plausible argument.

If I'm going the whole hog and want a fantastic piece of Super Content, I would telephone interview and web survey and desk research. The three together are very powerful and combine the best features of each.

Other ideas I've seen work very well:
- Walking the floor at an industry exhibition, stopping people for quick fire questions and quotes
- Handing out a short questionnaire at your own event/forum
- Posing questions direct to groups on LinkedIn and other forums
- Taking insight from facilitated discussions at either your own events or those run externally
- Hosting a round table discussion and writing up the discussion and insights.

A Onefish Twofish client recently ran 'pre-research' with very senior level people about high level industry issues, using their comments to pepper the more specific, issue-led white papers with throughout the year. This had the advantage of reaching out to very senior people, setting the top level context and leveraging their name in the resulting papers. If you have the time and the inclination, this is a really nice idea.

Collate and interpret your insight

Ok, this is the hard part. I'll make no bones about it. Being faced with an array of data is daunting, so I like to use a very structured approach.

If you have lots of data and a big budget plus enough time…
With time and budget on your side, I recommend starting with the data, analysing it carefully and looking to see what this throws up.
- Create a spreadsheet and put your qualitative interview data into it. Code the responses according to a) topic and b) response. Ideally set this up so you can filter by interview question, topic and response – this will make it easier to eyeball.
- Use pivot tables (or manually create graphs) to analyse the quantitative data. Create cross tabulations wherever you think there might be a connection, for example asking "Of those who agreed that ABC was critical, how many used XYZ and how does that compare to those that didn't think ABC was critical?"
- Pull your desk research together into topics and juxtapose with the primary research.

Then pop a towel over your head and read all the information over the course of one to four hours (depending on how much data and time you have!).

Next, create what you think the overall story is and the three to five supporting nuggets might be. Lay these out in a document – they form your main sections as a storyboard. Drop your headlines and supporting data and quotes in there.

This is the time to take your suggested approach to internal stakeholders for approval. They will probably want the storyboard plus supporting material (raw data) presented in an easy to review format.

Now you're ready start to building your story out of your core ingredients, or hand this over to a content editor to do the actual writing.

If you have a modest amount of data and not much time or budget...

If you really don't have the luxury of time or budget and there is not an impossibly large amount of data, I recommend starting with the end in mind.

Scan the data and make some judgements about what you want the story to say.

Create an overall theme (likely to be your original headline or something similar) and create sections within this that either logically build the story around the headline or form three to six individual themes within the overall story.

Decide on the key messages for each section. Now, dig into your data and find what you need to support these messages. Pull data together and juxtapose it to tell your story. Find quotes which back up your points of view. If you haven't already got some great statistics from your desk research, search the web specifically to find what you need.

Create your content
You should now be pretty close to creating a first draft of the whole content. You'll need to do some writing (possibly quite a lot of writing!) and you'll also need to present the information in a very readable format. Whether you're going

for quick-flick magazine-style or traditional book-style, there is always scope for presenting information clearly.

Ideas for making content jump off the page:
- inset boxes with key statistics, quotes or questions
- schematics
- imagery, for example head shots of interviewees next to their quotes, or logos of contributing companies
- tables, for example 'Old School Thinking vs The New Approach' or 'Projects which fail tend to... vs Projects with succeed tend to...'
- two column format (a larger left hand column for the body and a right hand column for quotes and statistics).

How to position your company in your Super Content

Clearly the point of Super Content is that it is unbiased and unsales-y. But you still need to position your organisation squarely at the heart of the matter, otherwise it's money wasted.

Here's how:
- include a line in the introduction or executive summary which explains why your organisation is committed to researching trends and how this topic fits with your overall offering

- add an About Us section at the end, positioning you as a leading provider and explaining what potential clients can buy
- pop a 'what next' section at the end, highlighting next steps they can take with you, if they want to know or do more
- insert an 'Our Philosophy/Position/Opinion' box at the end of each section to give yourself a chance to express your own point of view on the data and insights

Examples to read and take inspiration from:
Download contrasting pieces of Super Content on the Onefish Twofish website for food for thought and inspiration.

Case studies

The Lead Generation Machine requires a piece of Super Content each quarter, plus a case study on a similar theme. The case study makes the link between the great knowledge, opinion and insight you have... and how that might work in practice for a potential client. It helps to underpin the whole machine itself and also supports the sales process, for example a sales person or consultant might package together a one-pager about a particular proposition (what you do), the super content (proof that you're the experts), a press article about your work (third party endorsement) and a case study (an example in practice). This is a powerful combination – it's difficult not to make an impact with a complete set like this.

The golden rules of case studies

It's all about the client, not about you. Sadly, no one wants to read about how great you are. They want to hear about how an organisation like their own has tackled similar challenges. So the case study has to do exactly that. You can just bask in the reflected glory.

Make it strategic. Start with the business challenge and make a clear case for why the product or service was needed. What would have been the risk of doing nothing? Then look at the functional issue you particularly addressed (unless your service tackles the whole business) and explain what needed to change. Finally describe what you did and, of course, the impact it had.

Use first person quotes. A direct quote from a client is powerful. The more senior the better. Don't be afraid to go 'one higher' than your current contact to get the most impactful endorsement.

Brand it and make the results tangible. Anonymous case studies without clear results potentially damage your reputation. They beg the questions: "why is all the important, credible information missing?" Get that client badge firmly on the case study, use direct quotes from named client contacts and put the results into numbers and specifics.

An example in practice from our own client base.

Client: Vybrant Organisation (a talent and leadership consultancy)

Business challenge: good solid growth, but needed to differentiate in a very saturated marketplace and move up the food chain – otherwise price erosion was inevitable and difficulty in achieving planned growth.

Functional challenge (marketing): positioning was no longer accurate and the marketing approach and material was supporting the old target market, not the new.

What we did: repurposed the brand, created more strategic/CEO level collateral, implemented The Lead Generation Machine.

The results: the number of new business meetings at a senior level rose dramatically and with it, new larger opportunities in the right target market, facilitating growth.

Practical tools: Case Study Interview Guide

Use the template below to structure your information and interview your client to create the perfect case study.

Questions to ask internally
- What was the challenge facing your client?
- Why did they choose you to deliver this initiative?
- What was the main objective of this project from your client's point of view?
- Did you achieve this objective and exceed the client's expectations? How?
- What was the business impact for your client on achieving this objective and post-initiative in general?
- How would you describe your relationship with your client and the manner in which you worked together on this project?
- What was the biggest challenge for you on this project and how was that overcome?
- How do you envisage this case study will portray your business? i.e. what are the main strengths/skills that you want to come across primarily?
- What is the best thing this case study says about you and the way you work?

Questions for your client
- What was the overall challenge facing the business that prompted this initiative?

- What were your key objectives for this project?

- To what extent were these objectives met?

- Can you describe the impact on your business post-initiative? *If this appears difficult to describe prompt the interviewee by asking for anecdotal evidence.*

- Why did you choose our business for this project?

- Did you encounter any unforeseen challenges with this project? If so how did we help you overcome them?

- What feedback did you receive internally regarding the project?

- How do you intend to build on the outcomes of this project? What's next?

Now you have some fantastic content, you're ready to create some noise...

Step Two:
Make some buzz

(get on the radar)

So many companies I talk to feel they could develop so much more business, if only people knew who they were. They're not just talking about incoming enquiries and a ringing telephone, they're talking about:

- Recognition when they make contact with potential prospects ("I've heard of you – you're the people who...").
- Credibility in pitches ("Let's go with Company ABC. They've clearly got the track record and reputation").
- More traffic around their business – more calls, a bigger and more inter-connected network, more visitors to their website, greater footfall on their trade stand so that their marketing budget is reaching more people for free.

We already know that reputation is nothing if it isn't positioning you in the right space. And the previous section on producing Super Content is a massive step towards this. In this section we're going to cover two major areas:

- Sweating your hard-won Super Content in every possible way.
- Leveraging other people's content automatically to become the home of all information and insight in your target market.

There are three areas you should be thinking about and we'll tackle them one-by-one.

- Your own website as an industry hub.
- Your social media presence.
- Your presence in the press and on the speaker circuit.

First stop: turn your website as an industry hub

If you're going to create some buzz, you might as well create a great big noise around your very own website, as a good starting point.

This means creating a site which potential clients can find easily (both via the natural search listings and through relevant site links and referrals), want to return to regularly and trust their contact details to.

Being found online

Search Engine Marketing is how we use the web to promote our business. A fundamental part of this is climbing the natural search engine listings.

This means increasing your site's visibility in search engine result pages (SERPs). Part of the process is updating and altering a website's content and code so it can be read by search engine spiders and ranked highly by search engine algorithms. What we're trying to achieve is more traffic through to a site via natural or organic search (SEO).

There are three main areas of focus:

1. Technical SEO - the code on the page
This ensures search engines can read and interpret your site content. Key actions are as follows, and you'll need your web developer's help with most of them:

- make sure the code-to-content ratio is correct
- add a Google sitemap if one doesn't already exist
- check your website meets the latest xhtml standards
- use cascading style sheets (all sites built since 2003 should use CSS)

2. Content SEO - relevant keywords in the right places, updated regularly

The objective for search engines is to consider content on your pages as relevant and therefore to rank the pages highly. Content is core to the success of any SEO initiative. Internal SEO covers the thought and process that must go into content creation. Google states that site owners should create a "useful, information-based site" and to "write pages that clearly and accurately describe your content". Here Google is stressing the significance of content. A page written around a key phrase focus will have an incredible effect on search engine visibility. Next to this, content naturally gains long-tail key phrase positioning that a site owner wouldn't necessarily target, bringing in qualified traffic. Adding other relevant pages will help as well: if you have more pages on your site, the more ways people have to find your site. If you have more relevant content, you will have more positioning opportunities. The more your site is considered a "resource" in Google, the better your site's visibility in search engine result pages (SERPs) will be.

Key actions are as follows:
- Conduct keyword analysis to determine which keywords your prospects are using to search for you and where you have the opportunity to stand out from the competition.
- Review title tags (the text that appears in the very top of your browser bar) and make sure they are keyword rich, descriptive and engaging.
- Use the right kind of html codes (e.g. STRONG for bold and EMPHASIS for italic).
- Make sure you are using header tags (h1, h2 etc) correctly and filling with relevant keywords.
- Fill the site with good keywords in the users' language, paying particular attention to internal and external links - the words you use here count for more.
- Use related links throughout the site to a) drive users around the site and b) boost your search engine rankings.

3. Public relations SEO - connecting your site to other relevant sites
Search engines rate the credibility of a site based on which other relevant sites link to it and how. As online strategy moves forward this particular aspect of SEO will become more important.

Key actions are:

- Start a link building strategy - if other sites with similar relevant content link to you, Google will rate you higher (particularly if they are a well trusted site).
- Create and distribute regular online press releases. They may or may not get picked up by the 'real' press but they can have a very big impact on your search engine ranking for specific keywords, plus (perhaps more importantly?) they help to craft your 'Google Home Page'. Specifically, when a prospect searches for your company in Google, what they see on the first page or two of results speaks volumes about your reputation and expertise, i.e. if you're not on the front page, you don't really exist. By placing articles all over the web with positive headlines and copy, many will make it onto the first few pages of Google for your company name and you're therefore controlling what people see when they search for you. Excellent.
- Set up profiles on a range of social networking sites including LinkedIn, Facebook and Twitter. Encourage your employees to do the same and link back to relevant content on your site.
- Blogs, wikis and RSS feeds are more popular than forums in search results - so comment regularly on other high-ranked blogs and create wiki articles.
- Bookmark your site on key social bookmarking sites including delicious, digg.com and reddit. Try technorati if you are a techie company.

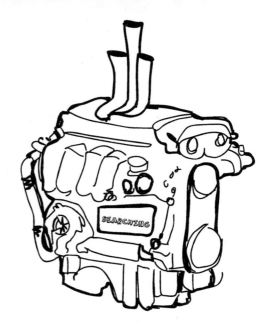

- Use video on your site - it's the most sought-after content on the web and it's set to increase in importance.
- Set your company up on a range of search engine directories - major search engines do pay attention to these and use them to validate data from your site.
- Make sure your business and all its offices are listed on Google Maps – it's amazing how many enquiries you can drive this way and how few organisations have got their act together on this one.

Be aware: successful implementation of any SEO strategy relies on a mixture of all of the above i.e. you might do well on the technical side of things but if you have bad content you will lose any of the gains you have made.

A bit more detail on online press releases

We talked earlier about how important online press releases were for search engine rankings and Google Home Page reputation. In case you're not already using this technique, here's how.

How to write the perfect online press release

Online press releases are virtually identical to traditional press releases that might have been sent to the newdesks of publications. My only philosophy is that you don't need such a good reason to run an online press release as you're not risking breaking an important journalist relationship by sending too much irrelevant copy.

Good times to post an online press release include:

- new product or service launch
- when you have something to say about an industry issue or development
- case study release
- white paper or other content release
- new significant team member
- new client win
- upcoming event (or debrief on recent event)
- award nomination or win.

PICK AN ANGLE!

The format we use to write press releases is roughly as follows:

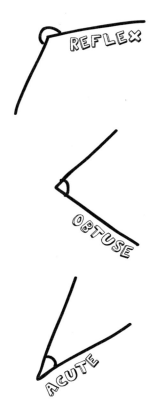

- Pick an angle (just one!) – make it newsworthy and market-focused.
- Create a clear, keyword rich, benefit-led title.
- Tell the whole story in the opening paragraph (the who, what, when where, why).
- Use this opening paragraph to create a 200-character summary for use later.
- Elaborate on the detail, using bullets to show results or list out important details where this is helpful.
- Use an example to illustrate the story if possible.
- Include a quote which adds something new (and doesn't just embellish or state the obvious).
- Insert any links in full .
- Add a boilerplate 'About Company ABC' in a separate section at the end.
- Finish with contact details, if they haven't already been included elsewhere.

Write the story as you would like it told by the press – just in case they pick it up and run with it with little or no modification.

Also, remember that the press are not your potential clients (even though we hope potential clients will read your press releases). They are looking for facts and angles. They are not interested in sales copy.

It (almost) goes without saying that it's vital to get permission from clients if you are mentioning their name, quoting an employee or giving any details about an internal project. I like to get this in writing (an email is fine) as quite often the person you receive permission from may be challenged on this later. It's good to be watertight and the same goes for case studies and anything else you might publish which includes client information.

Example online press release: the successful press release from our first book

New book teaches B2B companies to make successful complex sales

UK B2B marketing agency Onefish Twofish has launched a new book: How to Sell Clever Things to Big Companies. The book is authored by Carrie Bedingfield, an expert in helping build a pipeline for complex/big ticket B2B sales.

The book is important because companies selling complex B2B goods and services often struggle to articulate their offerings in a simple and clear way, leading to a loss of sales. Numerous B2B companies have used the concepts in the book to create a strong pipeline of leads and sales.

The book provides fresh insight on the full range of core issues facing B2B companies:
- how to build trust-based relationships when most contracts are 'jobs for the boys'
- how decision makers think – and three ways to get their attention in a noisy world
- defining your most profitable target market – the race you can win
- packaging up what you do so that it's super-easy for prospects to buy
- creating a website that truly generates buzz and new contacts for B2Bs
- spreading your marketing risk: the top down and bottom up approach
- using innovative approaches to break into hard-to-reach companies.

With a fresh and human style, the book is full of insight and practical 'how to' guides for organisations trying to crack into large new companies and contracts. As an experienced and innovative marketer, Carrie Bedingfield is well-placed to offer tried and tested methods for success.

How to Sell Clever Things to Big Companies is available at www.onefishtwofish.co.uk for £15 plus P+P.
Press: to request a copy of the book, please contact jenny@onefishtwofish.co.uk

About Onefish Twofish

Onefish Twofish is a B2B marketing company, focused on selling complex or intangible services to big companies. Working with 50 fast-track companies each year, Onefish Twofish creates and delivers strategic marketing campaigns. As a full service agency, the business positions companies in the most profitable space, generates new opportunities, nurtures leads to fruition and creates powerful brands with creative and knowledge-based communication.

www.onefishtwofish.co.uk

About Carrie Bedingfield

Carrie Bedingfield is a bright talent in B2B marketing. She founded Onefish Twofish aged 25 and wrote her first book before reaching 30. Working with a wide range of fast growth companies and growing her own business rapidly, she has developed a systematic method for building B2B businesses. Carrie is available for press and TV interviews.

Good places to post your online press release:

There are so, so many of these and a quick Google of 'free online press release distribution sites' will reveal a plethora which are likely to be more up to date than my list below. But here is good starter for ten to get you off a blank page.

www.pitchengine.com	Free
www.prlog.org	Free
www.pr-inside.com	Free
www.pressreleasepoint.com	Free
www.newswiretoday.com	Free
www.ukprwire.com	Free and paid options
www.przoom.com	Free and paid options
www.24-7pressrelease.com	Free and paid options
www.transworldnews.com	Free and paid options
www.pr.com	Free and paid options
www.freepressreleases.co.uk	Free and paid options
www.pressbox.co.uk	Free

Other things to do with your press release:

- Post it on your website
- Tweet it
- Diggit, Reddit etc
- Post it to LinkedIn (your status, your own group, groups you are a member of)
- Submit to online PR distribution sites
- Send to relevant blogs – contact via the link on their website
- Distribute to offline media channels – directly email relevant journalists
- Send and email to prospects or clients sharing the press release (don't call it a press release in a client facing email; call it a latest news update or something similar)
- Add it to your next newsletter.

Creating a sticky site visitors want to return to

When we visit a site, why do we go back? Unless it's a site we just think is super-cool, we go back because we get something valuable from it. If we think in consumer website terms, there might be information that keeps us ahead (like moneysavingexpert.com). It might be the best place to find new information (like the BBC). There might be a database of articles, which we dip into regularly (like timesonline). It might allow us to connect with peers (like Facebook or LinkedIn). Or perhaps there is a tool, search engine or widget we use regularly (like rightmove.com).

As B2B marketers, we need to look to our bigger-budget cousins in B2C for inspiration. Hopefully the examples above have already sparked off some ideas. Here's what they spark for me.

- Could your website aggregate all the best articles in your industry (including your own) and provide them in a searchable format? Visit www.talking-talent.com > Resources for a good example.
- Is there a tool, survey, calculator or search engine you could incorporate into your site?
- What about a forum which discusses a particular issue, or a member area which allows similar companies and people to connect?
- Could you bring together the very latest information in such a way that the market comes to you first? For example, this could be share or currency prices, times in different time zones, a calendar of industry events. The dream is that you put something so new and useful on your site that visitors check it virtually every day.
- What about webcasts and podcasts – if the role as industry article hub has already been claimed by a competitor, could you dominate the same space, but using a different media. For example you might consider creating a range of How To webcasts or Industry Guru Interview podcasts

At the very least you should have a really good article bank which you add to regularly. We call ours Ideas not Articles or Resources because that's what we're trying to provide - and few other competitors seem to use the same approach. You could have a How To section or an In Practice or Best Practice page, or even a Toolkit landing page. This is the place your Super Content should live, so it makes sense to shape the page around these big serious pieces of content you're producing.

Making it easy for people to 'stick' to your content
If some of your content is restricted access, make it very simple to register, very easy (or automatic) to log back in on a subsequent visit and ensure that all the content can be accessed through a single log in (so if you want four articles you don't have to register four times).

Link up to other systems visitors might be using, for example provide an RSS option, connect to Google Reader and whatever other widgets are newly available since this book went to print.

Flag fresh content on the homepage (automate this with a news feed if possible) so that it's easy to see what's new.

An idea: *the Website Open Week*
Here's a technique we've used with great success in the past. If your main articles are restricted access only (or better still, if you have some paid items), you can create an open week where you open up a different section of the site to unregistered guests each day for one week. You can promote this heavily beforehand and then send an email out each day, promoting the content freely available that day. You're encouraging

I'M STUCK BUT I LIKE IT

people to visit five days in a row and to sample your content. If you can leave the very best item(s) behind bars for the whole week, you will still get some sign ups (and therefore leads). But you can be sure you will have created a massive buzz.

Sticky like glue: *the power of creating your own diagnostic tool*
I love, love, love using diagnostic tools to create buzz. They can be fiddly to create but once you have them, you have a fantastic tool which you can use in so many ways.

The principle is to host a really useful tool that helps a prospect understand their issue better and what their options are. Every time someone uses this tool, you get their contact details (and they have provisionally self selected themselves as needing your services so are half way qualified). You also receive the data they inputted which you can use at an individual level to follow up with each lead and also at a group level to feed your Super Content. In fact, with a bit of thinking, you might be able to feed your quarterly Super Content purely through diagnostic tool completions – which would be nice!

The practice goes something like this:
- Find an issue or question that your potential clients would value an answer to and which directly leads to identifying a Market Need Gap (a quantifiable gap between what clients need and what they actually have right now).
- Create a formula or way of quantifying their issue, diagnosing what they should do about it and ideally valuing the benefit of your recommendations.

- Set up a questionnaire or input area online where visitors plug in their unique information.
- Create the report structure so that the visitor inputs lead to a unique report that diagnoses their issue and suggests a solution.
- Promote this throughout your marketplace to generate as many completions as possible.
- Follow up each lead with the offer of a conversation and more detailed support and advice based on their data.

Some good examples I know work really well:

The Carbon Footprint Calculator www.carbonfootprint.com/calculator.aspx

The Equiteq 7 Levers Of Growth Assessment www.equiteq.co.uk/equiteq/DisplayArticle.asp?ID=18272

The 4SL IT Landscaping Profile Tool www.4slconsulting.com/itprofiletool_intro_screen.aspx

The Ethicability Moral Character Profile www2.ethicabilitytest.org/prod/user/welcome.php

Your online and social media presence: what you should be involved in and how to go about it

Where to start. So many tools, so many options, so little clarity about what actually works. The reality is that none of us have plumbed the depths of creating an online buzz yet. We can't categorically say that Twitter does or doesn't 'work'. My philosophy is that there is a range of really good core activities that will work for most businesses. These are what we test and implement with our clients, with some exciting results. We trial new things on a test basis, not wasting client time and money until we know for sure that they will generate a return.

Before we start, these are some of the questions we ask.

- Research, research, research. Know your customer — where do they go online? What sites do they read? Sounds obvious, but you want to be found there too.
- Do you have the amount of time you need, and the resources to ensure it's successful? It can be a big time-suck. Who will do the work? How much time will they spend on it each day?
- What goals are realistic? What does it mean to "own the online space" in your market? How will you know when you've achieved this?

And we make sure clients are on board with the core principles:

- Don't feel that you have to be on everything - just do the things that will give you results depending on what you want to achieve.

Automate everything you can, for example RSS feeds, sourcing content through Google Alerts or using programmes such as Tweetdeck to help you keep track of all your Twitter accounts at once.

The core online tools (or places you should be)

LinkedIn - your professional Rolodex. (Think of Facebook as the personal one.)
- Used as a public profile so people can find out about you and build credibility.
- A method of getting in touch/networking with people.
- Use LinkedIn Groups, one centred around your company and one centred around your industry, to network with similar people – a bit like an online professional association.

How to put it to good use:
- Link in with every prospect, client, influencer you can find. Look out for contacts that move organisation in the news feed - you can email them to congratulate them and suggest a meet up! Without LinkedIn, these people would drop off your radar.
- Update your status from time to time to reflect some of the exciting things your business is doing - this is currently underused, so yours will stand out.
- Join all relevant groups (turn off the comms setting if you're getting bombarded with nonsense) and start your own groups. Post questions and useful articles around once a week.
- Search for relevant but currently cold contacts using the search function. Invite these people to join one of your groups.

Twitter - used by your prospects as a way of keeping in touch with what's going on in the industry (by 'following' the updates of companies they find interesting like yours and sharing website links about things of interest with their contacts).

- The most popular form of microblogging.
- Originally a social tool, but rapidly transforming into the perfect business forum.
- Once you sign up (free), you can a) 'tweet' your own short messages (usually pointing to a relevant article, tool or trend) and b) follow other people's tweets.
- Great for pushing your website up the search engine rankings and building a 'following'.

How to put it to good use:
- The key is to provide value by sharing interesting links etc (go to www.tinyurl.com or bit.ly to shorten a link so it fits within the 140 character limit of each message, or "tweet").
- It can be time-intensive so don't feel that you have to be involved in it all the time!
- It can be a good way to get an "in" through direct messages with people who might not be willing to talk to you otherwise.
- Use bit.ly to track the links you post (bit.ly shortens your links so that they fit within the character limit and also enables you to track how many people have clicked them).

Google Analytics – not strictly a social medium in its own right but a tool you install on your website to find out how many people visit your site and what they do when they get there.

- Ask your web developer to set this up on your site and check it at least monthly.
- Consider using prospectvision.net to make invisible visitors visible for £250 a month (a lot more than free, but well worth it if you can contact 5-6 companies a month who are searching for a supplier on your site).

Blogs – function as an online newsletter to help you build credibility as well as providing content to keep contacts updated with your name (and lovely keywords to boost your search engine ranking).

- Short articles from 100-300 words commenting on a new development in the industry, talking a little about an aspect of a methodology you use etc.
- You can make the content work hard (aka 'sweat') by reusing it as a newsletter and emailing it to your contacts every few months.
- It creates credibility around you and what you have to offer – by sharing a little of value, people trust you. Posts should hardly ever be straight adverts for your company – perhaps no more than 1 in 10.
- Posts are hosted on your website, as fresh content improves your page rankings.
- Create the newsletter as an email with short snippets of content, with links back to the full content on your blog/website, or as one really good article you can email to your 'warm' contacts list.

How to put it to good use

- Blog weekly or monthly - as much as you have the time for. Pick one subject/slant and discuss. It doesn't need to be War and Peace.
- Use posts to feed your newsletter.
- Tweet new blogs and post them on social bookmarking sites (see below) to increase exposure.
- Visit others' blogs on similar subjects, make a comment and link back to your original post.

Social bookmarking (Digg, Reddit, Delicious etc) – a method for sharing useful information online

- Links submitted to social bookmarking sites are 'voted' on (e.g. 'dugg') up or down.
- The most popular links are viewed by millions of users.
- Especially useful to improve your page ranking within Google. Plus these are probably the best suited to casual browsing for useful industry information.
- Social media isn't something you do just to get on the bandwagon, so to speak – pick the particular result you want and do the activities which will lead to that result.

How to put it to good use

- Sign up with Diggit, Reddit and Delicious (free).
- Post your blogs on each and hope they get dugg/red/delicioused!
- Make sure your own site is registered on each - get every member of your team to sign up, log on and add your site with keywords. A great help for SEO.

Monitoring the big wide world out there

We've talked a huge amount about how to get messages out there in the online world. The gaping omission is that there is so much listening we should be doing too. And the web holds virtually everything we need to know about our market place.

Listening can be a time-consuming, needle-in-a-haystack type activity unless you put some good tools to use.

Here's a selection of some of the better listening tools and how you might consider using them:

Google Alerts – an essential piece of kit for marketers and sales people. You can set up keywords that you would like to track and Google will email you when a new piece of content which matches your keywords comes online. Choose from an instant update or a daily/weekly summary.

- As an absolute minimum, set up an alert for your company name and any product or service names so that you always know when something is published about you.
- Set up some broad keyword matches to keep track of overall trends in your market place.
- If you're regularly tweeting or maintaining a LinkedIn group, consider keywords which will alert you to new articles you might want to tweet about (for example I have "b2b marketing tips" arriving in my inbox daily – there are usually 2-5 that are worthy of tweeting or posting in my LinkedIn group straight away and that allows me to stay on top of these 'maintenance' jobs).
- Set key account client names as keywords so that you can track what's happening for key clients on a regular basis.

RSS feeds via Google Reader – a good way keep an eye on the broader marketscape. Companies who regularly publish articles often create an RSS feed that website visitors can subscribe to. It's essentially a list of the most recent articles and takes the form of a piece of code, accessed via a link. There are lots of things you can do with RSS, but for listening purposes RSS makes keeping up with new content on a range of sites really easy. If you use an RSS reader such as Google Reader, you can subscribe to all your favourite sites from one place and check all the new content together, instead of having to visit every website separately and work out what's new. It's simple and clever, even though it sounds slightly techie.

All you need to do is use your normal Google account (or set one up if you don't already have one – it's free) to log into Google Reader. Then follow the instructions to set up RSS feeds for your favourite sites. You can also set up a Google search as an RSS feed so you are monitoring what's new in general on a particular topic as well.

Twitter – the ultimate instant listening tool. I love to listen on Twitter. Among the gibberish, there is bang-up-to-date, short and sharp insight. Type in a keyword and you'll see what people are saying about the topic right now. You'll also be directed to the best of the articles on the web. If something is happening in the moment (whether it's a new software release or the fact that LinkedIn is down), Twitter is the place to listen.

Step Three: Generate leads

(make the invisible, visible)

Now we really get down to business – generating leads is what the Lead Generation Machine is all about, after all.

What we're talking about here is uncovering opportunity and making invisible market potential, visible. If you've got the first two steps in the process firmly under your belt, you should have built up some good latent demand. Now let's turn it into pipeline.

We're going to talk about two main lead generation activities.
The first is active lead generation. This is about proactively getting out there and asking for opportunities. It's targeting people and attempting to engage them directly in a conversation.

The second is passive lead generation. Having built up the traffic on your site and the buzz around your organisation, the next step is to convert as many of these into real conversations as possible, making it super-easy for browsers to become buyers. Until these people make themselves known to us, we can't nurture them and we have to rely on them making all the moves. So passive lead generation is about providing every possible opportunity for suspects to hop over the fence and become visible prospects. The nice thing is that if you get this right, you can watch the leads flow in at a very economical cost-per-lead. Perfect.

Active lead generation

Let's start with active lead generation. Many companies come to Onefish Twofish having built a business on word of mouth and referrals. This is great (and to fail to do well from referrals probably means you're doing something wrong) but it's only part of the story.

Businesses with a growth agenda should absolutely be reaching out directly to potential clients and creating opportunity.

Key principles

Getting stuck in and successfully asking for opportunities requires:

Repetition: hearing the message or receiving the request a number of times ultimately commands attention. Don't be afraid to be persistent – but don't be insistent. I like to use series to make sure I've covered ground before moving on to a new list – for example a set of three communications over a five week campaign, followed by a four month break and then another set of three.

Consistency: building trust is best done in consistent layers. Your communication should be consistent over time (e.g. from one piece of direct mail to the next) and between items (e.g. between an email and a landing page). That doesn't mean you can't break the rules and grab attention – but within a structure and context that the recipient has learnt to understand and trust.

Imagination: being quirky for the sake of it is rarely a good plan, but using imagination and creativity to bring your communication to life in a way that tells the story even more clearly is always a good thing.

We also need to think differently about what constitutes a lead. Rather than trying to dig out people who are already looking for the solution you provide, active lead generation is about creating that opportunity from scratch – specifically, helping companies to understand and value the extent of their problem (or missed opportunity) and then showing how what you do enables them to make or save money.

This means starting much earlier in the demand curve and deploying education campaigns, not just pure lead generation activity. Though this might mean more effort and a longer sales cycle, it can close out other competitors quite nicely and build strong, reciprocal relationships – and it's definitely the way the market is moving. Prospect expectations about how much you will support them during the sale are rising all the time. You're right to match or outpace this; otherwise your competitors will do so ahead of you.

With this in mind, here is a range of campaign ideas for you to mull over and tweak for your own purposes.

Campaign one: This Is A Cold Email

The idea: go straight through the radar to decision makers. Ask for what you want. Simple and surprisingly effective, this campaign is designed to take you from cold email to appointment (or sale, if that's more appropriate in your sales cycle).

What is it?

It's a campaign based on three emails. Each email is designed to look like a personal email, from you to the recipient. Everything about the email should ensure that it is not instantly labelled 'sales email' and deleted. It should almost feel as if it's from someone the recipient knows, in look and feel, if not in content.

The three emails are clear and direct – and they ask for a meeting or a sale. They acknowledge the fact that they are direct emails. They get alongside the recipient in the most straightforward way possible: "You are probably thinking about ABC, we sell XYZ, should we be talking?"

Step one: write and send an email that asks for what you want, in the most straightforward way possible

Step two: Make sure the email looks and feels like a personal email, even if you use a widget to send it (no images, fancy signature or footers).

Step three: Follow up with two more emails, acknowledging the previous emails and asking again for what you want.

Like many campaigns, this one is quite admin-intensive. Given that the email is designed to look as personal as possible, it doesn't look too good if you send a 'personal' follow up to someone who has already responded. So you'll need a razor-sharp eye on the detail: ideally someone who is personally responsible for the campaign, manages the data cleaning end-to-end, and can eyeball the data and spot problems rapidly.

Depending on the size of your company, market and average sale, you might consider a format like the following.

- Buy or rent a list of 6,000 suspects.
- Run 1,000 of this list through the 3-email campaign each month.
- Each suspect will therefore go through a campaign every six months (assuming they haven't responded sooner).
- If this works well and data is available, scale up the campaign in volume to achieve a great return on investment.

Campaign two: The Webinar Web

The idea: high-value content that is easy to create and attracts potential clients like honey!

Webinars are great. If you haven't attended one as a delegate, do so very soon. If you haven't run one, you'll find they are surprisingly easy to deliver.

The reason I like them so much is not because I imagine that all your prospects are wild about webinars (they're not). It's because they are so easy to set up and so easy for prospects to bite on. You'll find you get lots of interest, if you promote your webinar well, without the hassle and cost of running a seminar or event.

Please understand that I'm not suggesting you give up running events, especially if they work well for you. In fact in our final stage (Nurturing), pressing the flesh is an absolutely fundamental part of moving prospects along the pipeline.

But for pure lead generation (making invisible contacts, visible), webinars can work very nicely indeed. If 100 sign up and only 10 attend on the day, you won't have egg on your face. There is virtually no expense so if you have to move or cancel a webinar, that's no problem. And they are so easy to sign up to. I think twice (or more!) about signing up to even the most interesting in-person events. But I register for webinars all the time.

That's why we call it the Webinar Web – it hooks people into your nurturing pipeline neatly and quickly. Plus it gives you great opportunities over the course of the marketing year to communicate with a particular target population, showcasing your expertise.

Step one: Create a webinar series – consider running one per month, or perhaps a series of three, repeated each quarter.

Possible formats include:
- A presentation based on your organisation's knowledge.
- A practical How-To session or tutorial.
- Showcasing a case study.
- An interview with a client or prospect (they might share their views or talk through a case study from their own organisation).

Step two: Set your schedule for the coming year, book interviewees (if needed), and find the right technology (there are lots of options but Webex and GoToMeeting are both excellent market leaders and worth the money in my view).

Step three: Promote before and after – double whammy. Send an invitation plus two to three reminders before the webinars. After the event, send debrief notes, slides, the podcast/webcast and a reminder of future webinars.

Step four: Integrate the resulting podcasts/webcasts into other campaigns and onto your website (perhaps requiring a registration to access – all the better for generating more visible leads).

Another nice idea: You can offer to syndicate your podcasts and webcasts to other organisations, websites and blogs. Editors are always looking for excellent, non-salesy content.

And a final thought: We like to partner up with similar but non-competitive organisations to deliver webinars. Both our databases are invited and we then get some nice cross-pollination where we can legitimately build a relationship with their contacts.

Campaign three: Typography Takeover Email Campaign

I think you might quite like this. No one is really talking about this technique (yet), but we've found it very powerful – and amazingly inexpensive and easy to run.

The idea: Create a series of three sequential emails that are html based, but use no images. This means they look fantastic in virtually every email client (and don't require the recipient to 'load images' before looking their best). Instead of imagery, use bold typography to give lots of personality and impact.

Step one: Devise your campaign in the normal way, targeting your market and creating messages and a sequence of emails.

Step two: Plan in a great (very short) headline, a slightly longer by-line and a clear, short call to action. These form the ingredients of your typography based design. Write normal body copy but keep it nice and short.

Step three: Get your web or design company to load these in, using over-sized fonts for the title, by-line and call to action. We favour Georgia, if your main font is serif, and Tahoma, if it's not. Both are excellent, web-safe fonts. You will need a designer to make this look fantastic – it's super-simple, but it's the design eye that's needed.

Step four: Load this into your normal email distribution system and off you go.

Campaign four: Never Approach A CEO Without A Big Idea

Earlier in this book, we discussed the Big Idea. If you remember, it's the visual, verbal and physical embodiment of your core brand concept (how you uniquely solve your customer's core problem). This campaign is all about using the Big Idea in the biggest and best way possible. When people talk about "creative", this is what they mean.

The idea: Create a campaign which lifts your offer right off the page either in the way it's delivered, the construction of the direct mail, or the visual signposting – whatever makes sense for your proposition.

Step one: Define your core message clearly.

Step two: Brainstorm with your team (or whoever you can grab!) and think widely and creatively about how to embody your message. Or, give your agency a brief and get them to do this for you. Bring together a whole load of ideas and then review them for efficacy (will they actually work?), face validity (will they work with your audience?) and feasibility (are they affordable and possible?).

Step three: create and distribute your campaign – and then follow up religiously! Creative stuff is a) usually more expensive and b) more disruptive, so don't waste the opportunity by failing to follow up with huge energy and discipline.

Campaign five: Crayon Me Beautiful

Stand by for a slightly more niche campaign we've run a few times with great success, but it might just spark an idea for you.

The idea: Create a 'hand-drawn' video for your business that visually explains what you do and why it's so special. As an added bonus – for a handful of your most special prospects – you can hand draw their logo (or the decision-maker's name) into the film – a big wow!

Step one: Create a storyboard of the message you want to get across. Keep it short and very clear.

Step two: Get your designers to mock up this storyboard and review to sign off.

Step three: Film an illustrator hand drawing your story, then speed up the film so the story is being drawn and told before your eyes!

Step four (optional): Include a frame at the beginning that draws the recipient's name and/or logo. They are effectively in the film. Incredibly powerful! You might consider creating customised versions for your 20 biggest prospects (just changing the opening frame to keep the time and cost down) and then a generic version for everyone else.

Step five: Incorporate this into an email campaign (or load onto a CD or memory stick for direct mail). Go fish for clients.

A variation. The clip doesn't need to be hand-drawn and filmed. It could just as easily be designed in Illustrator and animated in Flash. We just like the hand-drawn version because it feels like you're drawing it for your client there and then.

The style could be playful – or more 'serious' for CEOs or senior manager level, and something that truly captures their attention.

Other places to use and sweat this video:
- Place on online video aggregators like YouTube and Vimeo
- Use as a banner or a landing page on your website
- Add it to your email footer
- Embed it into a proposal PDF with 'click to play' functionality.

Campaign six: My Very Own Landing Page

The idea: Used in combination with one of the above, this campaign involves creating a unique web page (with a simple log in) for each campaign target. This page contains (or seems to contain) material specific for them and a welcome note written personally from you. Good for a small number of large potential clients, with multiple targets in each.

Step one: Consider the needs and issues of your target market. What would they find most helpful or impactful? If you could link them through to a personal landing page, what would it ideally contain? Some ideas to get you started:

- a diagnostic tool with some of their details pre-completed
- a top level, external review of some aspect of their business (obviously, in a way that's related to what you sell) – for example, Onefish Twofish could create a simple review of our prospects' websites and post this on their unique page
- a collection of the most useful articles for their organisation or industry or project.

Step two: Build the landing page template. You could either commission this as an add on to your own website (not hugely expensive, especially if you use a modular Content Management System as we do for all our clients at Onefish Twofish, allowing addition of this kind of module at the click of a button. Well, almost). Allow comments, if possible, so that the prospect can respond quickly with questions and interact with the information you're providing.

If your own website isn't really geared up for this, sign up to an online tool which will enable you to do the same thing on a hosted server. My favourite is Google Sites (a completely fantastic tool for so many projects and purposes). You can throw up a clean, sharp site, almost instantly – and for free (even better). Plus all the functionality you could ever need is already there.

Step three: Choose your targets and populate their pages. The ideal is that there is content which is core to all of them and that you only tailor certain, simple areas, to make the setup as efficient as possible. Create a simple log in formula for each (e.g. username equals their company name and password equals their own name).

Step four: Use one of the other campaigns to grab attention and encourage prospects to visit their site. This can work particularly well for multi-stakeholder sales as a variety of stakeholders can view the same, up-to-date information in one place.

Step five: As you build your relationship with this prospect, include all the info they might need into the site. For example, if you send them a proposal or quote, add this to their site. If you send them some 'saw this and thought of you' articles, add them to their site. We like to put our call notes and action lists up there too so they are transparent and viewable to the potential client. It gives them a taster of what we might be like to work with (hopefully organised and completely open). And it makes it feel like we're starting a project already – it closes the mental gap to us running an actual project for them.

A lower-cost, lower-effort but equally creative variation: If you don't fancy creating something from scratch and tailoring it for every single prospect, but you like the idea of homing in on a very small number of large prospects, try creating a "We want to talk to you" page on your site. This page would include the logos of all the companies you want to sell to (six to 20 feels about the right number) plus a clear, bold statement about why you want to work with them. This is a very confident way to chase a corner of the market. It does have some obvious downsides, for example making your target list publically available and potentially putting off those who don't feature on your list. But for some marketing campaigns, this will be no issue at all and the benefits of being able to opening target a prospect will far outweigh the disadvantages.

Tips for brilliant campaigns

Include a 'what we do' statement on whatever you send out. This orientates the recipient, builds trust, puts the campaign into context and might even provide a cross sale. Pop it somewhere noticeable but low down in the visual hierarchy.

Make your call to action incredibly clear and simple. Stick with just one if you possibly can. If you have multiple calls to action (for example you have a series of assets or resources you are offering) group them into one section called 'Downloads for you' or a more suitable title.

Personalise your campaigns. 'Hi Jane,' gets a better response rate, tests show. But you need nice, squeaky-clean data to do this; otherwise you'll end up with 'Hi [first name],' or 'Hi Peterson J.,' by mistake.

Make your URL super-clear. If the recipient is even halfway interested, they will want to look at your homepage. Make your main URL clear and obvious (and clickable if it's an e-campaign).

Sell – but with openness and good sense. We're all mugs if we provide oodles of great content in our campaigns yet no clear direction for the prospect on what they can buy from us to solve their problem. At Onefish Twofish we treat selling as a very straightforward activity, and our campaign work is no different.

HI JANE!

OH HI!!
DO I
KNOW YOU?

YES!

Here are some of the ways we might sell in our campaigns in a straightforward way.

- Include a side bar section called 'How to work with us'.
- Add a call to action to the end of each content section such as 'Contact the client director for this project to book a telephone discussion'.
- Insert a section called 'Take The Next Step' – this might include further downloads they might be interested in, an event they might like to join and of course a direct contact.
- Hyperlink relevant phrases throughout the campaign copy (obviously e-versions only) to relevant pages on your website.
- Use specific names of contacts in your Call To Action. This will improve your response rate and also provide a rough tracking mechanism. If you're really going for it, you could include their picture and a 1-line bio to truly make the connection between the contactor and contactee. It's up to you.
- Run a pilot and test. It can feel like a drag, but it's almost always time well spent if you are running any kind of sizable campaign. Multi-variate testing is great for the really big boys, but for simplicity and the ability to create data I can take real decisions on, I prefer:
  - Straight A/B testing – comparing two variations of an email, Call To Action, landing page, subject lines, send date/hour or any other important variable. Clearly, it's best to change one thing at a time.
  - Incremental testing – we almost always stage campaigns so we can test and refine 'in-campaign'. This means releasing the campaign in batches and continually refining details so that the response rate improves throughout the campaign.

Tips specifically for email campaigns

- ***Getting past the spam filter*** is the number one job (otherwise all your hard work goes to waste). Make sure your copy, code and images are not going to make you fall at the first hurdle. Try www.emailreach.com for a subscription service or www.mailingcheck.com for a free service.

- Get more for your money by ***including 'read more' links throughout***. Recipients want to scan, take in the whole lot and then click to what they want (that's how we think online).

- Make sure the important clicks and ***calls to action are within the standard preview pane*** and not 'below the fold' – don't make your recipients work for it.

- Include a ***physical address*** – always. Be legitimate and within the law.

- Think about how the campaign will look on a ***mobile or PDA*** – so many people filter their emails before they even hit their laptops. Consider creating a version specifically for PDAs. The first 25 characters of this email version are the most important.

- ***Use images sparingly*** – email was never designed for them. Image-rich emails rarely do well in a B2B context. My feeling is increasingly that emails have to stand on their own two feet, even if the 'load images' button is never clicked. This will inevitably have an impact on your open rate as many will read the email without triggering an 'open'. We call this a 'false negative open result' – they read it but it looks like they didn't. However, your click rate should remain the same (or go up, ideally).

TOP TIP: don't let your design agency persuade you to do an image-led, highly creative email campaign. It just won't work with a cold audience (though it will have far more success with people who know and trust you already). Every time, the sense is 'This is such great creative, it's worth breaking the rules in this instance'. I promise you it isn't. Be strong!

- Use the identifiers wisely. Subject Line and Sender are two crucial clues we scan and use to categorise the email rapidly: Useful or not useful? Spam or ham? Read, file, respond, forward or delete?
- Market research shows people are more likely to open the email if they recognise the sender's name – so an individual name works well in the Sender box. I also quite like [Company Name – Contact Name] (e.g. Onefish Twofish – Carrie Bedingfield), provided it's not too long. I think it's best to use a real person's email address but I would recommend you create a variation for this person, so you can manage list cleaning and responses. For example carrie.bedingfield@onefishtwofish.co.uk instead of my regular email address which is carrie@onefishtwofish.co.uk. I can provide access to the former for an agency or team member who can then work through all the responses outside of my regular inbox. It's also great for tracking as you can use a couple of variations to help track campaigns.

TOP TIP: if you're using multiple mailboxes, make sure you manage those endpoints very tightly. I have known the most fantastic leads arrive 6-8 weeks after the campaign finished, only to be missed, as the mailbox was no longer being checked regularly.

Tips specifically for direct mail campaigns
- Hand address your envelopes. Unless you're sending more than 10,000 in total, I promise you it's affordable and the improvement to response rate is totally worth it. Find a temporary person with lovely handwriting and the time and inclination to do a repetitive task.
- Seal envelopes with a sticker or stamp. Printed envelopes just look like spam and also that you've spent too much money. Sealing with a sticker or stamping with a stamp you've had made is a great way to add your personality. It's cost effective but with a great return on investment.
- Use coloured envelopes. Find (or commission) envelopes that match your brand or have a coloured lining.
- Use a creative address label. Create a branded address label onto which your addresses are either written or printed. This kind of detail can have a big impact.

Passive lead generation campaigns

Campaign one: Knowledge based Google Ads

The idea: High value content, peddled via Google Ads to cut through the race for clicks.

Step one: create or adapt a piece of high value content.

Step two: put it on your website, behind the simplest of forms.

Step three: set up Google Ads with relevant text and keywords.

Step four: set a budget and get going.

Step five: follow up, test and measure response.

In practice: the Onefish Twofish ideabook

We created an ideabook: a 12 page how to guide with real tips and tricks that people could access straight away.

We advertised it on Google: 120+ people a month downloaded it for around 6 months.

- Total cost to us over 6 months: £600
- Total responses: over 800
- New positive relationships: 48
- New clients: 8
- We think we'll convert another 10-12 over the next 2 years
- And... an introduction to the Thames Valley Enterprise Hub
- And... 14 referrals.

Total estimated value to Onefish Twofish so far - £145,000

Following up – techniques for getting the very most out of each campaign

- The no pressure 'classic' email -> call technique. "Did you get the information? What's your feedback?"
- Start the dialogue straight away. We send a 'Did you find what you were looking for?' email.
- Automate this process over three weeks with a set of scheduled auto responses.
- Stage your emails: send one on Tuesday and then a follow up on Friday, referencing the first.
- Cross sell. "If you liked this, you might also like..."
- Follow up people who clicked and ask the right question: did you read it, like it but not manage to do anything just yet?
- Add every response to your ezine list. Make sure they get a regular top up of your wonderful wisdom.

Step Four: Nurture prospects

(automate the process of cherishing your crown jewels)

Leads that are nurtured before going to sales buy more, require less discounting, and have shorter sales cycles.

There is a great lead nurturing agency in the States and their first task is to value your leads – they call it Weighing Your Gold.

It goes like this.

1. Calculate your average deal (tricky, I know – but we can all have a stab at this, using the average first deal as a nice conservative measure if that's the simplest way).
2. Guestimate your conversion rate – for every ten companies or contacts who enter your universe and know who you are, how many could you turn into new business, if you followed up brilliantly with every one?
3. Total your house database – those people you have permission to market to.
4. Multiply the three together, for example £50,000 average first deal size x 5% conversion rate x 2,000 contacts = £5,000,000.
5. Now cast your mind forward to the lifetime value of these contacts, not just the first deal value.
6. Finally, gawp at the potential value of your current database (and the immense weight of your gold).

Have I convinced you that it's worth investing in building and nurturing your database?

There are lots and lots of ways to nurture leads but the best ways are effective and as automated as possible. We'll talk about these first, and then move onto some slightly more personalised and higher investment ideas for your very special people.

Here are the three automated ways to nurture your leads we recommend most highly as part of the Lead Generation Machine; a quarterly newsletter, as-it-happens sweating emails, and a quarterly event.

A quarterly newsletter

Though I hate the word 'newsletter', I love the concept. Regular, fresh, valuable content which keeps you front of mind, cross-sells, encourages referrals and builds your brand. What more could you ask for?

But it's fair to say that both hard and soft copy newsletters have been rather overused. If we've read 'Welcome to our Spring newsletter!' once, we've read it a zillion times. This kind of Newsletter-For-A-Newsletter's-Sake leaves me as cold as it does you.

So the trick is to take a completely different approach. Here are the 10 commandments of effective newsletter writing. Flout them and join a thousand other wasted words in the spam folder...

1. *Don't call it a newsletter*

I hate newsletters. You hate newsletters. So don't call it a newsletter. See Commandment 2 for alternative ways to describe your newsletter.

2. Make it useful

At work, we focus our time on activities that provoke thought/interest; make us look good in front of our boss; help us do our job better, or save time/effort on an existing activity. We're in survival mode. If your newsletter doesn't tap into at least one of these, it is unlikely to survive.

Classify your newsletter into a high business-value communication which clearly signposts it as being for your particular niche e.g. Small Business FD business bulletin, Change Management Monthly Resource Book, Managing Sales Teams: Inspiration and Insight.

For example, one of our client newsletters is titled 'Ideas for Inspirational Leaders: 60 seconds on...'. As it's pitched to Director/CEO level, we make it clear it's for their level and highlight how quickly they can 'onboard' the new idea.

The idea is for a member of your target audience to consider it so useful to their work, they just HAVE to subscribe.

3. Theme each edition

Unplanned newsletters can be a bit of a random jumble of whatever information is easily gatherable at the time of publication. This is confusing for the reader and not very memorable. By planning themes, you will signpost the great content much more clearly and also leverage future topics at the sign-up stage.

Let's take the Change Management newsletter as an example. Possible themes might include: effective change programme communication, stakeholder management, project management, avoiding typical derailers, measuring success.

If I was a Change Manager I would be much more likely to subscribe to a newsletter which clearly laid out the content of upcoming editions. And when I received the newsletters, I would read more of each of them, knowing they knit together into a comprehensive concept.

4. Use regular features

The theming concept works well in partnership with regular features. This means a layout of article types which is repeated in each edition. These might include a thought article, an interview, a top tips section, a news feed, a case study, an interactive poll etc. The format depends on the focus of your newsletter.

A trick gleaned from successful magazines is that regular features help the reader navigate and quickly absorb the information as well as keeping their interest, edition after edition. To avoid 'me-too-ism' make sure you create sections that will work well for your content and give them interesting names. For example in the Xancam newsletter, we call the interview section 'The Big Three' and ask each VIP three killer questions on the topic for that edition.

5. Turn content gathering into prospecting

Use the process of pulling together content as an opportunity to engage with your target audience. For example if you have a very senior and strategic contact who is difficult to sell to (or to get on the phone for that matter), you could interview them for an article. It always surprises me how willing scarily-important-people are to speak when they know they're not being sold to.

If you're feeling particularly brave, why not pitch to a number of people you haven't met but know by reputation. Tell them you think they'll have something useful to say on the subject and would they consider contributing a quote, a piece of insight or a tip? With just five of these you've got yourself a pipeline – or at least the potential for one.

6.   *Don't oversell or undersell*

Ok, there are two ends of the spectrum to avoid. At one end is a pure advert. At the other is a newsletter full of fascinating content, all provided for free with no indication of the company behind it and what they do.

Steering a course between advertiser and sucker can be tricky – here's how:

- If you have something very relevant to sell on the back of the theme, you can insert one advert for this. But it should be in the style of 'find out how to...' rather than 'buy it here!'.

- Always include a 'call to action' at the end of each click-through.

- Make sure that as many sections as possible link through to something on your website.

- Once people have clicked here, they will often click around to find out what you do.

- Include your contact details and a short description of what your business does in every newsletter.

- Make sure all content links clearly to something you do. Be wary of writing anything which is interesting, but doesn't conceptually link to something you can sell.

7. Absolutely, positively no parish news

We've all done it, but we can definitively confirm that parish news makes you look small, inward looking and local. So no matter how great the Director's wedding photos are, or how fun that Fun Run you all did for charity really was, keep it out of your client newsletter.

The only exception is if you can tie it clearly into the theme. But the link should be good and strong. Not tenuous (and definitely not tedious).

8. Make it look fantastic

There are lots of awful looking email newsletters out there – mostly created by non-designers using online newsletter building tools. If you refuse to pay a designer to lay out each issue for you, then the bare minimum is to use a system like NewZapp which will create a really solid template in your branding which makes whatever you add look good.

A key issue is monitoring how the newsletter will look in the preview pane, before the images are loaded. At this crucial download/don't download stage, the newsletter has to look great or the decision will not go in your favour. Some recipients will read newsletters without ever downloading the images – so if yours is readable without images, so much the better.

9. Build your subscriber list

Size isn't everything, but the larger the number of the right kind of subscribers the better (obvious really!).

Optimising the organic growth of your list is a given. This means having a clear sign-up page (with all your forthcoming issues listed, plus examples of previous editions) on your website. Add 'calls to action' which link to this page from everywhere you can think of: your email signature, relevant articles on your website, other people's newsletters, forum signatures, marketing collateral, press releases and so on.

Proactive growth of your list is optional – but it can be the only way to get started. If you have a list of people who already know you one way or another, send them a 'premail' explaining that you think they would be interested in your newsletter and that they can subscribe/unsubscribe below (your choice as to whether you force them to opt in, or opt out). You can do the same with cold contacts – but expect a far lower response rate. Don't deploy 'opt out' for cold contacts – only opt in.

We have worked with organisations who just send their newsletter to bought lists and wait for people to unsubscribe. Technically this is not spamming (as long as it is a business email address, there is a clear unsubscribe option and you are using a list which permits this type of communication). However, this can often be perceived as spam with important brand implications – so treat this course of action with caution.

10.   *Be proactive with the clicks*
Your newsletter provider should furnish you with a clever report explaining who opened your newsletter and who clicked each link. If your newsletter is non-salesy and insight-based, then any direct selling on the back of clicks will be poorly received (e.g. Hello Mr Burns, Big Brother tells me you innocently clicked on an article in our newsletter just now – I am now going to assume you're happy for me to enthusiastically sell our services to you). So don't do this.

However, a bit of clever and targeted follow up can work wonders, for example, a follow up email to those who clicked on a particular link e.g. 'If you liked this article, you might be interested in our webinar on 24th April'. Or a follow up call for feedback to those who downloaded something e.g. 'I saw you downloaded our white paper and wondered if you'd give us some feedback when you've had a chance to read it'.

Think about frequency...

The Lead Generation Machine lends itself to quarterly editions, timed to release the Super Content created on a quarterly basis. In line with our theme of doing a few things really, really well, quarterly is a nice pace – regular enough, but not so frequent as to be onerous. Coming up next are 'sweating emails' which are shorter and more frequent. They plug the gaps between newsletters quite nicely.

Having said all that, there are some exceptions, if you produce a different kind of content. For example, if your newsletter is more of a timely update, you will obviously want to send it out in a timely way (Weekly? Monthly? As it happens?).

A few examples of newsletters which lend themselves to a more frequent schedule:
- Weekly external article round up. At my previous company, we used to create and send The Big Three each week – the three most important articles in the industry that our network should know about. Weekly was a great format for this.
- Latest results. If you have devised a newsletter format which updates your network on the latest results from your database or the latest figures from your industry, this will work much better if it's as timely as possible. If you're a recruitment consultancy, this might be

'latest candidates'. If you're a company broker, this might include 'new companies listed to buy'. You get the idea.

- Blog. We discussed blogs earlier, the conclusion being that if someone in your business loves writing them (and writes good ones) then go for it. It you are in this happy situation, blogs should go out weekly or monthly. Otherwise, they are just articles.

...And also about format

I'm often asked the question: hard copy or electronic copy (or both!)? There is a relatively simple answer to this.

You should always, always run an electronic copy as a minimum. This is cost effective, viral and trackable. The electronic copy should comprise a number of intros to articles or content (called 'stories') with clear calls to action in the form of links to read the full content/download the PDF/register for the seminar/whatever else you might be asking people to do. This means you can fit all your content in a readable, scannable format in one email and you get the benefit of all that lovely clicking which will record in your email distribution software. If you reproduce an article in full, you've no way of knowing whether it resonated with your audience or not.

If you have the budget and your audience is right, consider a hard copy as well. As punters, we get far fewer hard copies these days. They are surprisingly 'sticky'. The format also allows for much more creativity, if not interactivity. Your brand can truly shine through, unconstrained by html and spam filters.

However, hard copy is significantly more expensive and can be very time-consuming (whatever you estimate for your internal time budget, double it), even if you outsource as much of the production, packing and posting as you possibly can.

Many companies we work with send an electronic copy to their whole database and then single out a proportion or warmer of more important prospects for the hard copy newsletter.

As-It-Happens Sweating Emails

In between newsletters, the Lead Generation Machine maintains ongoing contact with Sweating Emails. Designed to drip feed high impact content to your newsletter list, these emails should be very short, client-focused emails, ideally in a plain text format (no html or fancy images and branding are needed). They should feel more like a personal update; a 'thought-you-would-like-to-know'.

The impact of sending these out is huge. You might just get a direct response in the form of a lead – a huge bonus. But more importantly, you are gradually building and shaping your reputation. You are increasingly looking like the place where good things happen.

The fundamental principle is to keep it short. You can send them fairly frequently (up to weekly, but no more) if they are short and sharp. If they are in the slightest bit detailed, they will rapidly feel like spam.

Timeliness is also important. The more rapidly you can send out your update, the more newsworthy and the less spam-like it will feel.

Make the logistics as simple as possible. A good Customer Relationship Management system (like Sage Act or SugarCRM or Salesforce.com) will enable you to produce and send these quickly and easily, provided you have set up your groups correctly.

Good things to write sweating emails about

- new client wins
- award wins (or nominations)
- articles in the press
- new white papers, case studies or other piece of great content
- new products and services
- new key team members
- a website launch or relaunch.

Here's an example of one we wrote for Xancam Consulting, when they featured in The Times.

Subject:

Xancam in The Times: David Cumberbatch reveals how to become a successful CEO

Body:

What does it take to become a successful CEO? Whether you're in line for the big job or are responsible for selecting the best candidate in your organisation, here are ten ways to maximise the chances of a successful appointment. Xancam's Managing Director, David Cumberbatch, points to a genuine desire to live the life of a CEO, strategic ability and passion as three key ingredients for a budding Chief Operating Officer.

Read the full article **here**.

And here's another we wrote when Xancam's CEO Dr Maria Yapp was listed in the top 25 thinkers in her field.

Subject:
Xancam's Maria Yapp is named in HR 25's Most Influential

Body:
Xancam's CEO, Dr Maria Yapp, has just been named in Human Resources magazine's Top 25 Most Influential rankings. She shares the top spot with Charles Handy, Lynda Gratton, Will Hutton, Lord Leitch and Dame Carol Black amongst other high profile names. This is the second consecutive year that Xancam's CEO has featured in the HR list of Most Influential. Maria's highest scoring areas were Commercial Relevance and Originality – powerful recognition of her contribution to high potential identification and development.

Find out more about the HR Most Influential list **here.**

Register to receive Maria Yapp's forthcoming white paper: Big Impact, Clear Measures - How Leading Companies Measure and Achieve a Strong Return on their Investment in Talent.

A quarterly event (not quite automated, but not too far off)

Events are really a must have. For all the great e-business, auto-contact, i-client technology out there, pressing the flesh (or the vocal cords at the very least) is still so, so important. If we think about creating a series of stepping stones that prospects can walk across to become clients, surely the actual meeting of minds/ bodies/voices is the minimum final step.

In the spirit of automation, events also provide the opportunity to meet lots of people at once, providing them all with the same great message and experience. So they are actually very efficient and somewhat automated.

There is a huge range of successful event formats. And I like to think up new event formats all the time as potential delegates value fresh formats which shake up their thinking and feel new and different.

Some tried and tested event formats to consider

- A half day conference with a range of external speakers, themed around a hot industry topic. Add in interactive sessions or 1:1s with your consultants for extra impact.
- A round table 'whirlwind' – six tables with a speaker/facilitator on each, working through a different topic. Sessions run every 30 minutes with a 5 minute break in between. Delegates rotate from table to table each time the new session starts, choosing the topics they are most interested in.
- A priced workshop (i.e. a day or half day tutorial which delegates pay for) which showcases your expertise – and pays for itself at the same time.
- Parties with bite.

A special shout out for webinars

We talk about webinars earlier in the book (The Webinar Web lead generation technique). They can be a good event substitute if you're short on time, money and resources, or if you just want to market test an idea or issue. The huge advantage (aside from the cost) is the lack of hassle and stress. No room to set up, no worries about how many will attend and no last minute panic about the vegetarian option...

Webinars are not a substitute for a face-to-face event – but given the choice of webinar or no event-type stepping stone, the webinar wins every time. A very handy tool to have up your sleeve.

Now get sales

(The art and science of selling from your machine)

Everyone's got to sell

The good news is, if you've created a good machine, you'll have earned the right to a conversation and created an access point with your target market.

The bad news is, you have the right to a conversation and access to the right person – but now you need to sell.

There's no way round it. We've all got to sell.

Happily, selling is the fun bit

It's the great conversation, the chance to ask incisive questions, have an opinion, make your potential client feel clever. It's the dance.

There is another whole book on selling to businesses just waiting to be written. In the meantime, here are my selling non-negotiables.

Be anything but a sales person. You facilitate conversations, you help clients think. You believe in abundance and are magnetic because you *don't* sell.

Be clear and straightforward. Ask for what you want (a meeting? an answer? whatever it is, ask for it).

Be persistent. They won't marry you the first time they clap eyes on you. Be patient and expect a journey. Don't make marriage the goal from day one. Make 'getting to know you' the goal in its own right. If they are The One, marriage will take care of itself...

What next?

(You look interesting. Come and tell us about yourself.)

We're all ears

I would be more than delighted if every single person who read this book emailed me (carrie@onefishtwofish.co.uk) to say hello. Or to tell me what they'd done with some of the ideas in the book. Or to tell me where I've got it completely wrong. You don't look like the shy and retiring type...

You could always have a look on our website

There are other fun things on our website (www.onefishtwofish.co.uk). You can watch videos and all sorts. If you're a very small business or start up, you might like our Small Business Ideabook.

Would you like some bread?

You can visit us any time at our office in Pangbourne, near Reading. We're five minutes from the M4, there's lots of parking and you'll always find a desk and an internet connection if you're passing. If you arrive around noon, you might just be in time for some home made bread or cake.

Onefish Twofish
27 Shooters Hill
Pangbourne
Reading
Berkshire
RG8 7DZ

+44(0)118 3217457

hello@onefishtwofish.co.uk

Thank you

(Team effort. Overflowing fishtanks everyone.)

Especially to...

Book fishies: Jon Matthews, Liz Hayward, Hannah Robertson, Sacha Brech

Kind relations: Families Hall and Bedingfield

Truly inspirational clients and colleagues: Alan Sears, Catherine Coale, Greg Davis, Paul Russell, Dr Maria Yapp, Tim Cray, Bill Ingram, Caroline Beard, Steve Dance, Kristin de Thouars, John Rosling, Dorothy Nesbit, Jo Stark, Richard Bovenschen

Fabulous friends: Jen Caldicott, Laura Newell, Neil Basil, Hannah Bussey, Andy Dilkes, Richard Burbedge.